GOD
IS NOT
SMART

Anthony-Lorenzo Brathwaite

God Is Not SMART

© 2014 by Anthony-Lorenzo Brathwaite

Published by Get Ahead Coaching

All Rights Reserved

www.anthony-lorenzo.com

Get Ahead Coaching

Printed in the United Kingdom

All rights reserved. No part of this publication may be reproduced, distributed, or transmitted in any form or by any means, including photocopying, recording, or other electronic or mechanical methods, without the prior written permission of the publisher, except in the case of brief quotations embodied in critical reviews and certain other non-commercial uses permitted by copyright law. For permission requests, write to author at the address below.

Disclaimer: This publication is designed to provide the reader with educational insights and personal experience information in regard to the subject matter covered, and to assist in your journey to dream attainment. It is sold with the understanding that it is your legal right to use this information; the author and the publisher assume no 'responsibility' for your actions.

ISBN: 978-0-9575526-0-9

Cover artwork by: Anthony-Lorenzo Brathwaite, Hedia Media Group

DEDICATION

I dedicate this book to those who have been historically hurt and presently in pain; to those categorised as educational failures and social outcasts; the stereotypically labelled and statistically challenged; and those who, despite these obstacles, still cherish an "impossible" dream. Know you can live the life of your dreams. Just remember, *"It's not about what they say you are; it's about who you believe you are!"*

In addition, I want to dedicate this book especially to my children. This book is part of a legacy that I am creating for you. Daddy loves you and has been praying for you before you ever blessed this earth. Not only are you a gift to me (and Mummy!), you are a gift to this world.

ACKNOWLEDGEMENTS

Listing the people I would like to acknowledge was a difficult task as there are so many who have inspired me. Despite my reluctance, I am going to attempt it. If you are reading this and do not see your name, please charge it to my mind and not my heart.

To God, my Dream Author - the one who has given me the faith to believe despite the impossibilities that surrounded me. Knowing you, God, has been my greatest accomplishment and everything else is secondary.

My heartbeat, my support, my motivation, my inspiration, my life, my love, my best friend, my angel, my all. The woman who decided to trust me, support me, and give me "Hope", and last but certainly not least, take my last name. Mrs. Lynnette Brathwaite... YOU ARE AMAZING!

To my amazing family, I would not change you for anything. I love you all! Mum, Dad, siblings, cousins, EVERYBODY I Love you all. A special mention to one woman whose virtue and wisdom has taught me so much over the years is my grandmother, Mrs. Beatrice Sarah Green. I love you with my whole heart. A big shout out to my extended family, The Hopes, a true force of nature lol love you.

To the place and people who have given me a great spiritual foundation, Hope Assembly Ministries, under the leadership of Pastors Thomas and Eunice Alamu. You have been a great source of support to me; I appreciate your love and prayers over the years.

To my Dream Assistants, whose advice and actions motivated me to make this happen. Kunlé Oyedeji you are my '24/7' - Always there, always open and readily available for me to access exactly what I need. I am grateful for the friendship we share; you are an inspiration and a huge motivational force to me. "It's a Feb thang". Owen Ikhimnwin, you are literally my brother and there aren't enough words to express my deep love for you. You are a genuine reflection of God's love. Eric Adjei, you are the person who prays me through. I call on you and you appear; my personal superhero, a true man of steel! Your best is yet to come. Gordon Healis, what can I say about 20 plus years of friendship we share? You are truly a gift from above and an amazing Individual. Thankyou for lending me your gift of creativity and sowing into my dream by designing the book cover.Tunji Ogunjimi, you are a man after God's own heart; continue to share your gift with the world. Simon Philogene, Samuel Alebioshu, Thank you for your continual encouragement, support and respective input.

To Kofi 'Kase' Hanson-Asiedu, thank you for initially editing and reviewing this book and investing in my vision. You are a blessing and I truly appreciate your patience and persistence. To Kathryn Rooney: your advice, insight, and editorial direction have been invaluable. Dr. Liji Thomas, thank you for being the missing piece and making this book come alive.

To those who supported me by writing endorsements, I am eternally grateful. A special thank you to one of the most energetic, real and supportive visionaries I know, Jackson Ogunyemi. You have blessed me by writing the foreword, and asked for nothing in return. You have given me more than you know.

To the mentors whom I have not met, but who have been a source of inspiration to me through the power of media, whose faith and exemplary living has encouraged me to live and be better…

- Dr. Martin Luther King Jr.
- Bishop TD Jakes
- Tyler Perry
- Oprah Winfrey

To all the 'Go Getters' who support me by quoting, tweeting and retweeting, sharing, liking and encouraging me in my endeavor to spread my #GetAhead message. I salute you!

Finally, if you don't see your name here, it doesn't mean you are not important to me; therefore I have created a very special blank space just for your name. _____ thank you so much for your support; you are the best!

CONTENTS

What Readers Have Said & Foreword — Pg. 7

Why Read God Is Not SMART? — Pg. 13

PART ONE: THE DREAM AUTHOR, THE DREAMER AND THE DREAM

1. The Dream Author — Pg. 19
   - The character of the Dream Author
   - God kind of thinking
   - Exposing the con artist

2. Freedom is Found in The Truth — Pg. 25
   - Get real with your truth
   - Life Out Loud (LOL)

3. If There's No Purpose There's No Point — Pg. 29
   - The purpose for everything
   - The big dream
   - Dream Pioneers

4. How FAR Do You Want To Go? — Pg. 35
   - The sixth sense
   - The dreamers' success formula

5. God is not **S**pecific — Pg. 39
   - Don't Fear The Facts

6. God is not **M**easurable — Pg. 45
   - No such thing as a perfect plan
   - God planning over good planning
   - Practice doesn't make perfect, it makes better
   - The heart of the matter is a matter of the heart

7. God is not **A**ttainable — Pg. 51
   - Dream Drains
   - There is no good reason for your lame excuse
   - Stretch yourself

8. God is not **R**ealistic — Pg. 57
   - Statistics Are Not Fixed

9. God is not **T**ime-Bound — Pg. 61
   - God is not Time-bound
   - Time to grow up
   - The process of time

10. God is not S.M.A.R.T.! God is Wise! — Pg. 67

PART TWO: GET UP, GET GOING & GET AHEAD - COACHING YOU TO YOUR DREAMS

11. The Dream Coach — Pg. 71
    - *What is coaching?*

12. Arise and Shine — Pg. 73
    - *Wake up*
    - *Pay attention*

13. Lights, Camera, Action — Pg. 77
    - *Action proves decision*

14. Watch Your Ass! — Pg. 79
    - *Dream ass-assins*
    - *Dream ass-istants*

15. D.U.M.B^{TM} People Achieve Their Dreams — Pg. 85

16. D: Is For... — Pg. 87
    - *Dreams are not microwave meals*
    - *How to be more diligent*

17. U: Is For... — Pg. 91
    - *Fight back*
    - *The power of words*
    - *How to be unwavering*

18. M: Is For... — Pg. 95
    - *Imagination has practical application*
    - *How to be a motivated person*

19. B: Is For... — Pg. 99
    - *Information that feeds your belief*
    - *(Be)lieving in (You)rself*
    - *How to believe*

20. D.U.M.B. is the New Smart — Pg. 105

21. Go Confidently In The Direction Of Your Dreams — Pg. 107

References

About The Author

WHAT READERS HAVE SAID ABOUT 'GOD IS NOT SMART'

'GOD is not SMART' is a timely classic from Anthony-Lorenzo. If you are spiritual this book is for you. If you need motivation this book is for you. Most importantly, if you are practical then this book is definitely for you. Anthony-Lorenzo has taken a set of relevant principles from a model most of us are familiar with, and has turned it on its head in a unique way. The book challenges us to think out of the box in order to live out of the box. It focuses on the importance of not just dreaming but dreaming big and taking the necessary steps to see your dreams become a reality in your life.

I would recommend this book to every book reader, go-getter and world changer. Not only will this challenge you, it will change you and those you come into contact with. I commend Anthony-Lorenzo for taking the time and effort over the months past to create a masterpiece that will be a focal point of change in the lives of many."

Kunlé Oyedeji *(The Cornerstone & Life Solutions)*

'God is not SMART', has been cleverly constructed and wisely written, for the benefit of everyone. It connects the work of God in the lives of humankind to the fulfilment of their dreams. This book makes it clear that God is very much involved in the affairs of men from beginning to end. It demonstrates the practicality of faith, hence why it is a much needed book for this generation. Well done Anthony-Lorenzo.

Rev. Thomas O Alamu (Senior Pastor – Hope Assembly Ministries)

"Man's attempt to figure out God as if it is a personality to learn, is still fascinating practice. This book can help explore partial divine possibilities, in effort to contribute to the goal of completing a more tangible truth about God."

Chaz Shepherd *(Actor, and Singer-songwriter)*

"When I first saw the title 'God is not SMART', I thought author Anthony-Lorenzo did not know God at all! But after reading the book, Anthony makes it very clear that God truly is not smart, but rather a Supreme-Genius and is ready, willing and more than able to bring out the brilliance in you, through your dream!"

Larry W. Robinson (*Author, Host of dailyinterviews.com*)

"This is a well written and constructed piece of work, which gives you insight into how you can dream again if you have lost or forgotten your dream, how you can bring back that dream and also make it live. This amazing book teaches you how you can achieve those goals and visions in life the God kind of way, giving you advice on how to go about it and never give up on you and what's on the inside of you. This is a manual for living or rather Glory Realm Living in order to Live Heaven on Earth, and it all starts with one step. Take that step today and start living the life God has for you.

The author is someone who has lived what he has written and practiced it daily, so he is a product of success. Well done to Anthony-Lorenzo for giving us this awesome, simple and needed master-craft in such a time as this, for this generation to wake up to their potential and living out their dreams."

Tunji Ogunjimi (*Founder - Glory Realm Ministries and Author*)

"The book "God is not SMART" is going to amaze so many people. It's a needed tool for this time and this generation. So many have lost hope and focus. I know that this book is the perfect re-directive for anyone looking to not only live again, but to DREAM again."

James Murphy (*National Recording Artist*)

"What an amazing and life changing book. Everyone should go out and pick this up immediately! Congratulations Anthony-Lorenzo, what a labour of love. I'm sure it will touch the lives on many, the world over."

Steve Jones (CEO of VGS&L Entertainment)

FOREWORD

Just before Action Jackson sent me the foreword to this book, I got a personal WhatsApp message from him at around 4:40am. Here it is, verbatim:

"What have you done to me? This book is anointed, it takes away the burden of HOW HOW HOW and it allows us to just BE BE BE to achieve all that GOD has placed in us. Man it all makes sense now; it's the difference between trying to skate on grass and skating on ice. I love a smooth ride, this book has just helped me RESET my mentality about SUCCESS, you've just unleashed a LION bruv, Kai! It's 4:36 am and I am writing like my life depended on it! Foreword is on route... Continue to be led by Him and not man. Proverbs 3:5 #iAmDUMB"

I hope that when Jackson reads this, he will decide not to annihilate me for exposing him, but I felt the authenticity of his message was moving. The following foreword is the formal extension of this message, which I know came from his heart. Here it goes...

"Yaaaaaaaaaaaaaaay! Wohoooooooooooooooooooo! At last!" This was the most appropriate way I could express myself when reading this book, a reaction that can only be described as extremely excited with a big sigh of relief. Every page of this book 'gave me life', and brought an overwhelming feeling of refreshment to my soul. As a motivational speaker and an entrepreneur, I am more liberated in my ideas, thoughts and thinking as a result of reading this book.

My profession often means I challenge people to go for their dreams with resolute determination. But one thing that experience has taught me with reference to my own goals, whether that was to lose weight, run the London marathon, or expand my business, is that nothing goes according to "MY PLANS". I knew my WHAT and I knew my WHY, but the HOW was hijacked by another force, covered by a blur of idealism. However, the most important thing is that I got there in the end; not as I desired, but as it was destined to.

This learning curve has helped build the foundation of my faith, by providing me with the knowledge that I don't have to know every part of my journey, and that's ok! But my job is to trust and I will be guided.

Reading *God is not SMART* reminded me of the many people I have coached and currently coach, who for one reason or another have not fulfilled their dreams, and I now know that it's because they were trying to be S.M.A.R.T. Even whilst reading the pages of this book, I had to pause, because I was prompted to text a mentee who wants to start a business, but has spent the last 2 years creating a logo. Yes! 2 years on the logo. "I am perfectionist" was his response; "I like things to be in a specific way." It saddened me to see them behind the bars of the perfectionist prison. So this is how I respond...

"If you plan everything, what part do you want God to play? Let God guide you on how HE wants you to build his business for you. LET GO and LET GOD."

I know who will be getting a copy of this book. I personally co-sign the message of this book, knowing that there is a MEGA VISION that God has placed in my heart - though I don't know how it will happen - but I am encouraged that just like the great pioneers who have gone ahead of us, some of whom are mentioned in this book, we must take that first step, and the magic will happen. Steve Jobs did it, Walt Disney did it, Nelson Mandela did it, now it's your turn.

This book will refresh and reset your mentality about your GOALS AND LIFE, and it will cause you to go forth and RELEASE all those exciting dreams you keep talking about. Give your family and friends a break from hearing you go on and on about the things you've always wanted to do, because after reading *God is not SMART* you will be empowered to just go do them. When you get through each chapter I urge you to move by faith and see how much you can accomplish. From now on I know I will not try to be "too SMART for my own good", I now choose to be DUMB and directed by the ultimate power that is bigger, bolder and better, than I am. WOW! I am in the zone right now; the energy surging through my mind is enough to light up a city. No more talking, it's time to TAKE ACTION; I hope you will do the same. This book is perfect for a time like this, where there is a ton of false information floating around, distracting people from being free. This book answers the question of "Why can't I do what I know I should be doing?" Enjoy the new journey that will liberate and elevate your life.

Action Jackson
(Motivational Speaker & Director, Fixup Enterprise UK Ltd)

WHY READ 'GOD IS NOT SMART'?

If I told you that you have something in common with Martin Luther King, Steve Jobs, Bill Gates, Oprah Winfrey and Walt Disney, would you believe me?

These people all had big dreams, and if you are reading this I am going to assume you also hold a dream. The question is, if they could live theirs what is stopping you from living yours?

I think I may have the answer; **you are being S.M.A.R.T!**

What Is S.M.A.R.T.?

This book uses the word S.M.A.R.T. to represent two things. One is its standard dictionary definition, which concisely means *"clever or intelligent", and most* importantly the renowned goal setting theory, pioneered by psychologist, Edwin A. Locke. The S.M.A.R.T theory which is an acronym that stands for **S**pecific, **M**easurable, **A**ttainable, **R**ealistic and **T**ime-bound. The popular mnemonic is often taken to be the right way to qualify and/or memorise our dreams, as in "our dreams must be 'S.M.A.R.T" in order for them to be possible. There are different variations of the S.M.A.R.T acronym, attributed to many acclaimed professionals and quoted in associated publications. However, the underlying principle remains the same.

The problem with being S.M.A.R.T

I have encountered the S.M.A.R.T theory in practice numerous times. I myself constantly struggled to concretise it, yet despite my repeated attempts to be S.M.A.R.T it never quite brought the results I desired.

Then it hit me, just as if someone had spoken to me and said, *"God is not S.M.A.R.T!"* This realisation stuck in my head and my heart for many years, refusing to leave me. I just knew that I had to put pen to paper and write to see what would happen. What you are reading right now is the result of that insight.

The S.M.A.R.T method is suited to business, professional and personal development goals. Certainly, its framework is sensible and its whole purpose was to enable people to clarify their goals through a series of steps, so they could solidify their progress. Ironically, however, it has often done the opposite. It has set up five insurmountable obstacles even before you were able to take your first step forwards. Let me explain this a bit more.

- **S**pecific - The obstacle of having to know everything
- **M**easurable - The obstacle of needing to calculate everything
- **A**ttainable - The obstacle of having to reason out everything
- **R**ealistic - The obstacle of having to conform everything to good sense
- **T**ime-bound - The obstacle of having to ensure everything works to schedule

'SMART' people can be limited people; especially if they do not allow their dreams to form wings, solely on the basis of not aligning with 'SMART thinking'. The danger that presents itself here is, potentially world changing dreams can be discarded upon the scrapheap of unachieved dreams or the grave yard of disappointment. This book can change that.

How to get the most out of this book

Despite the book's motif of faith, it is not for 'religious' people. It is for anyone with a dream who refuses to settle for the mediocre and the mundane, and repeatedly contemplate breaking free from the prison of ordinary but without much progress. You owe it to yourself to try again and see what this book can offer you. It's different! The content is not meant to offend anyone, so please read with an open mind, understanding its context, so that you can get the most help in actualising your dream.

What you are about to read could make the critical difference between living out your dreams and living on a dream. It presents an alternative set of ideals that will challenge the customary paradigms, the traditional mind-sets which society has imposed upon us, and limit us. If you are ready to explore the whole concept of faith, put confidence in your higher power and believe in yourself, it is my heartfelt conviction that this book could radically change your life.

Whether this change happens depends only on you and whether you deliberately and consciously take onboard the concepts, and constantly practice the principles and axioms I offer you. Once you do, you will trigger off an extraordinary progression within yourself. Your approach to life will be proactive; and you will boldly take charge of changing your circumstances rather than being controlled by them.

Right now nothing in your life may make sense. Take heart, for you are at the crossroads, and this is the ideal starting position for a dynamic change which will reset the course of your life. Of course, no one at the beginning of a journey knows all that is going to happen. But as you go on, things assume clarity and direction. The only fact you need to know is that the principles in this book work. They are not altered by your personal belief or religion. If you still don't believe me, I challenge you to just go ahead and read. You may be surprised to find yourself a believer soon!

"A book is a device to ignite the imagination."

- Alan Bennett (Author and Playwright)

"Too SMART for your own good!"

You must have heard someone say, *"You're too smart for your own good!"* Usually this means that you are so cocksure about what you know that your very knowledge can turn against you, keeping you from being effective or successful. However, in another sense, it can also mean that you try so hard to make your dream S.M.A.R.T. that you find it hard to even start. The graver issue is that these five SMART areas only deal with the outer physical areas, ignoring the spiritual and/or internal obstacles that most people struggle with.

These include traps such as procrastination, low motivation, a lack of willpower, and a glaring deficiency of which underpins this book, faith.

In an attempt to explore these problems, I have split my book into two parts.

Part 1 – The Dream Author, The Dreamer and The Dream: This section takes a close look at the character and mind of God, so that we can find out why He gives us the gigantic dreams that He does, even when He knows that they are 'beyond' us. I have done this by uniquely exploring God's character as set against each letter of the S.M.A.R.T acronym.

Part 2 - GET UP, GET GOING & GET AHEAD - COACHING YOU TO YOUR DREAMS: This section offers further practical applications of what comes with the first step and every succeeding step towards your dream. To help you with this, I have created an acronym which runs counter to the S.M.A.R.T theory, called D.U.M.B

You could read this book in one sitting, since it is not very long. However, I suggest you think of it like a tool, rather than a novel, and use it when you need it. If you are really thorough and want to get the most from this book you may want to heed the following:

- Scan the chapters of the book, so that you can get a feel for the books texture

- Work with the book, i.e. periodically take time to reflect, write down your thoughts and continue

- Use the book repeatedly as a reference source, especially when considering working on other dreams

"Some of life's most amazing treasures are right before our eyes, but we fail to recognise them, because we're afraid to take a closer look. If you dare grab a magnifying glass and look over your blurred Snellen chart, you'll discover that God is not SMART; and that's a priceless illumination"

- **Anthony-Lorenzo Brathwaite** (Author)

PART ONE: THE DREAM AUTHOR, THE DREAMER, AND THE DREAM

1. WHO IS THE DREAM AUTHOR?

> "...The Dream Author creates and gives us dreams that... defy human logic and understanding; they are far beyond our normal reasoning..."

Just in case the title wasn't plain enough, I want to let you know that God is a major factor in this book. A big dream can only become viable if we first grasp the idea of a big God. There are many attributes of God, and a multitude of titles used to try to define Him. To some, God is Allah, Buddha, Jah or Creator, depending on their personal or religious belief. Then, of course, some do not believe in any higher power. They may possibly believe in the power of self or in other philosophies such as "What goes around comes around", which is the concept of Karma. In Christianity, He is called Jehovah, Yahweh, or in Hebrew, El. To simplify and draw a line under this powerful entity, I will use the term God or by my personal reference, 'The Dream Author'.

THE CHARACTER OF THE DREAM AUTHOR

If you believe in God, you already know that His various names are just some of the countless ways to describe him. These descriptions are word pictures of what He's really like, or His attributes. For example when we say God is merciful, truthful, and loving, we are expressing traits of His character with which we have become acquainted.

An author is defined as the maker of anything; creator; originator: the maker of something. An author is a common synonym with someone who writes a book or novel, or the source of a literary work. God not only authored the universe and all that is in it, but indeed "wrote" and inspired the creation of one of the world's bestselling books to date.

The book includes various life principles, motivational messages, and all the tips for successful living you could ever need. It works like a training manual, and includes compelling true stories of many who experimentally verified that the Dream Author's methods work. Quotes from this marvelous work will be used throughout God is not

S.M.A.R.T and you will see it referenced to as The Dream Author's Manual.

"My Book is useful for teaching, for showing mistakes, for correcting, and for training character, so that whoever follows Me can be equipped to do everything that is good"

– The Dream Author's Manual (adapted)

TAILOR MADE DREAMS

When we talk about God giving us big dreams, it is essential to understand that His intent is not to play a sadistic trick on us, by arousing discontent and empty longings within us just for his own amusement. We know this because that's simply not the way He is. As we come closer to Him, we understand how He plans for us to live a life of success. Of course there is no true definition which fully encompasses His nature. We are just trying to understand Him a little better so that you can gain greater insight into who He is and what your dreams mean.

The Dream Author is constantly creating, constructing, and distributing dreams to us. He sends us dreams to guide and counsel us, to establish His promise to us, and to warn or advise us.

"For God speaks... In a dream, a vision when sleep falls on people..."

- The Dream Author's Manual

The Dream Author's Manual, as well as other historical and modern materials, is replete with anecdotes of people whose life turned upside down because of a dream. Think of the Biblical figure Jacob, who had a dream one night in his wilderness sleep. In it, he saw God's distribution channel - angelic figures ascending and descending a ladder. The ladder itself led from heaven to earth. Let's not go into its theology right now; just use your imagination to picture it this way. Heaven is God's production plant where he is creating marvelous and original dreams precisely engineered for you. Moreover, He'll use any means necessary to deliver them to you.

Side note: For those readers who don't identify with religion or any religious group in particular, do keep an open mind, and even better, an open heart, to the concept of a higher power, or at the very least, a higher level of thinking. Think of God as your conscience. The conscience guides, directs, and can warn you off from what is wrong to what is right. That sounds very like God to me. Be open to embrace a wider view of the world and of the things around you.

"You need to look at life from a different perspective... sometimes"

THE GOD KIND OF THINKING

God means us to turn dreams into reality. However, the biggest mistake we make is waiting for God to make it happen. What we really should do is rely on God to help us act and make it happen for ourselves. You see, to realise a dream, you may need to invest money, a great deal of attention, and, more than likely, a whole lot of time, among other things. This can be a damper. We tend by nature to procrastinate, to put off actualising our dreams. Instead, we perform menial jobs that bring us the supposed comfort, security and stability of a steady income.

This is an immature and unfruitful attitude. As I have grown in body, mind and soul, one of the biggest realisations that hit me was that you don't have to wait for conditions to be perfect in order to make your dream come true.

But there are some things that you cannot be sure of. You must take a chance. If you wait for perfect weather, you will never plant your seeds. If you are afraid that every cloud will bring rain, you will never harvest your crops…So begin planting early in the morning, and don't stop working until evening. You don't know what might make you rich. Maybe everything you do will be successful.

– The Dream Author's Manual

The basic reason why we never get around to translating so many God-given dreams into reality, even apart from our natural fears and risk calculations, is the appearance of doubt in the mind. We tell ourselves, "God would never give me this kind of dream," or "This dream is too big; it's almost impossible. It can't be for me." I will discuss how to deal with this kind of mental block later. Right now, let me just say that the issue here is never with the dream: it's with the stinking thinking.

The person with a God-given dream must recognise that man's thoughts and methods are very different from those of God. They are on opposite sides of the spectrum. The Dream Author does not operate by our rules. The Dream Author creates and gives us dreams that, even at the best of times, defy human logic and understanding; they are far beyond our normal reasoning. In short, there is a way a man thinks, and then there is a God kind of thinking - and God does not think S.M.A.R.T.!

"I don't think the way you think. The way you work isn't the way I work... For as the sky soars high above earth, so the way I work surpasses the way you work, and the way I think is beyond the way you think."

- The Dream Author's Manual

EXPOSING THE CON ARTIST

"Do not conform to the pattern of this world, but be transformed by the renewing of your mind."

- The Dream Author's Manual

This mind-blowing advice straight from the Dream Author's Manual tells us not to conform to a specified pattern – not just any pattern, but the iron mold of prevailing social standards, attitudes, and practices. We are to stand apart from what appears to be the 'norm'.

Let's just concentrate on that word 'conform' for a minute. You can easily make two separate words out of it – 'con' and 'form'.

Con: To persuade by deception, or cajolery. To swindle; trick. The abuse of confidence

Form: Something that gives or determines shape. A particular condition, character or mode in which something appears.

Do you see what I see? The word itself suggests that there is an all-pervasive thought process, stemming from the media, education, social background, cultural influences, etc. Sometimes this produces good results, but at other times the consequences are terrible. This is the process that has helped to make you who you are right now.

For instance, are you the kind of person who says, "I can't" at the beginning of every sentence? "I can't be a lawyer, doctor or a millionaire because of *(insert excuse)*"? A person whose entire life revolves around satisfying the expectations of others? A person for whom beauty is defined by weight? One who thinks dreams are for the elite few?

If this sounds like you, guess what? You have been con-formed! So ask yourself what exactly shaped this thinking. Was it the media? Was it your parents? It could even be that proverbial red devil on your shoulder telling you "you are not good enough". In any case it's not really important what or who it is – because they are all wrong! At the risk of sounding trite, let me repeat that you really can do whatever you set your mind on. There are millions of famous achievers to support my claims.

The Dream Author's Manual goes on to use the word 'transformed'. The word 'trans' is a Latin prefix for 'beyond, across, through, and to move from one state or position to another.' Transforming is all about undergoing a change in form, appearance, or character. The age-old example of the butterfly which starts off as a blind crawling caterpillar but metamorphoses into something totally different is still unrivalled. The creeping form with so many limitations becomes a colourful, winged, butterfly, unlimited and unrestricted to roam wherever its wings take it.

Unlike the butterfly, our change is not so much in the physical. Transformation, for us, begins with the choice to learn all over again, in order to take a "bird's eye view" of life. Learning is essential for survival. If you are not learning, you are not growing. To fulfil your dream, it is vital that you make a radical shift in your thinking, or what I like to call an extreme mental makeover.

"The illiterate of the 21st century will not be those who cannot read and write, but those who cannot learn, unlearn, and relearn."

Alvin Toffler (American writer and Futurist)

If you have a big dream, you will have to do some things that don't seem smart. You might opt to go back to school to pick up necessary skills; you may choose to apply for a smaller job that moves you closer to your dream; or you might give up your job to start your own business. Regardless of what your big step may be, this book is about helping you to start. But for the process of relearning to take place, we must first reassess our understanding of God, especially in relation to our dreams.

2. FREEDOM IS FOUND IN TRUTH

Many years ago, a friend said to me *"Anthony, it's not how many years you live that matters; it's the life you live in those years."* That statement made a profound impact on my life and set something free within me. The truth is you could die at 27 or 97, but whether your life was relevant or not depends on what you did with it. If you live to 97, many would say, "Wow! Isn't it great to have lived so long?!" Yet, after you pass on, what story will appear after your name?

This reminds me of a popular television show which I used to watch in the '80s and '90s. It was called "This is Your Life". In every episode, somebody, usually a celebrity, would be surprised to find out that their life was going to be reviewed on TV before the public. In a capsule, the show would present their memorable feats - what they had done with their lives. You may not be a celebrity, but your life is telling a story. So don't fall for the popular belief that long life in itself is a worthwhile goal. To have nothing to show after a century of earthly existence is almost as if you had never been.

"It is not enough to have lived. We should be determined to live for something…"

- **Leo Buscaglia** (Author, Motivational Speaker & Professor)

GET REAL WITH YOUR TRUTH

You will never get ahead if you do not get real with the person you are today. This means to acknowledge and accept what and who you are when your mask is off; it is not your Twitter persona or Facebook profile or Instagram celebrity. Your real self is the person living inside, that reflection in the mirror, with your pitiful flaws, embarrassing failures and chronic weaknesses, but also great strengths, amazing potential and marvelous possibilities.

Every single one of us has a personal truth. This is what we truly believe about ourselves when nobody else is watching. It could be either a positive or a negative reflection, but the key is that it's authentic. Taking a truthful survey of who you are today is vital if you want to visualise the kind of person you want to be. That picture will help you prepare for the required change with insight and courage.

LIFE OUT LOUD (LOL)

In contrast how often have you heard it said, "Life is short"? Well, a quote from The Dream Author's book reads:

"What is your life? It is even a vapour that appears for a little time and then vanishes away."

- The Dream Author's Manual

To put it differently, we need to recognise that we have only a little time here on earth. There's no guarantee that tomorrow will ever come. This is not to spread gloom and despair. Indeed, I intend exactly the opposite! I want you to realise that you cannot control time, but you can control the way you use time. An online article about British Formula One racing driver, Lewis Hamilton, the youngest ever Formula One World Champion, was entitled *'Lewis Hamilton just happy to live the dream'*. What made me interested in the article was how the writer candidly described the Hamilton family in terms of their belief in God. The following is an excerpt:

"The family (Hamilton's) has also talked, a little more than some would like, about destiny and being blessed by God. Anthony said that God had guided Lewis through the last few races of the season and over the finish line... Plenty of sportsmen talk about faith, but his rivals, and others, have detected a degree of presumptuousness. Is Hamilton, they ask, the only one touched by God? If such talk of blessings and gifts points to a stunning self-certainty possessed by Anthony and Lewis, we must also acknowledge that, without it, they might be working in office jobs in Stevenage."

There are people who wake up to living a dream instead of allowing themselves to be imprisoned in a job merely to pay the bills. Since you are reading this book, I assume you want to be one of them! The

Dream Author gives you dreams to show you that we are not here merely to exist, but to live.

Don't waste your time on useless work, mere busywork, the barren pursuits of darkness....It's a scandal when people waste their lives on things they must do in the darkness where no one will see... Make the most of every chance you get. These are desperate times!

- **The Dream Author's Manual**

To live Life Out Loud is to live without regrets, unapologetic for having a dream and living it out to the fullest. It is to climb to new physical and spiritual heights, which are unknown to the multitude. This life speaks so loud that it grabs the attention of even the most absent-minded individual. It is so colourful it puts a rainbow to shame. It's so bright that darkness hides. This life is on the other side of fear, waiting for you to come and embrace it.

3. IF THERE'S NO PURPOSE, THERE'S NO POINT!

> *"A life without purpose, a dream without reality, even a career that doesn't have a goal is ultimately... unfruitful"*

There often comes a point in life when you wonder what it all means. You start to think that life has to mean more than chasing down temporary highs, or seeking something new to satisfy your thirst. This throws up some common questions such as:

- What am I here for?
- What is my purpose?
- What am I supposed to be doing to make my mark in this world?

The reality is many people have been there. Some linger at the crossroads, soul-searching, hoping to reach a point where the answer will resonate in their minds with complete conviction. They know that until they do, life will always be like taking a bus journey, paying for the privilege but never reaching the destination. The reason for this emptiness is...LACK OF PURPOSE! If there is no purpose then what is the point of living? That question is purely rhetorical, because the answer is none. A life without purpose, a dream without reality, even a career that doesn't have a goal is ultimately disappointing, unrewarding, and unfruitful. Living without a sense of purpose is a pointless existence because deep down, there will always be an empty space.

THE PURPOSE FOR EVERYTHING

"To everything, there is a season, a time for every PURPOSE under heaven."

-The Dream Author's Manual

Everything that exists does so for a purpose - and that includes you! Purpose gives meaning and direction to life; it lets you identify goals and determine what is important. Purpose releases the power to enjoy life and not just endure it. Once you choose to commit to your real purpose, your life experiences will take on a completely different form, as you see things from a different perspective.

How do you identify your dream? Well, a dream from God is quite different from your own dream. Our dreams are typically based upon selfish motives and ambitions, driven by negative ideas. But a God-given dream transforms not just us but also our world.

The Dream Pioneers whom we are about to watch in action had huge dreams. They had dreams that were not just for their own benefit. They did not set out to become a colossal success. They lived to make a difference, compelled by love and a fundamental dissatisfaction with the world around them. Their success was the inevitable by-product of their obedience to their life purpose.

"All successful people men and women are big dreamers. They imagine what their future could be, ideal in every respect, and then they work every day toward their distant vision, that goal or purpose."

- **Brian Tracy** (Motivational speaker and Author)

Another way to recognise your dream is that it will be closely related to your life interest and passion. This includes the thoughts that constantly pass through your mind, whether asleep or awake. They all point toward your purpose. I could even dare to say that any God-given dream is your life purpose in pictures. Now ask yourself, "Do you star in your own movie?"

THE BIG DREAM!

To clarify, dreams within the context of this book represent one's aspirations, goals, aims or ambitions. All these words mean the same thing: your dream. Your dream may come to you as a sequence of images, thoughts, or emotions presenting themselves to your mind while you're asleep. But it can also occur as a vision when you're wide awake, which I call a 'daydream'. Daydreaming is a short-term detachment from your immediate environment, during which your contact with so-called 'reality' is changed and partially substituted by a visionary fantasy, especially one of a better life. At that moment, your actual reality is in the hopes and ambitions you see in your imagination.

Dreams come in an assortment of shapes, colours and textures tailored to each individual recipient, and hold the power to change and define your ultimate reality. The average person doesn't know it, but each dream is a seed planted in your heart by God, and not by coincidence. Once that seed germinates into a fully bloomed tree, it produces an abundance of delicious fruit which humanity can benefit from.

The next important thing to establish is what is your big dream? Starting your own business and becoming a millionaire, or being a best-selling author with books that help transform the lives of millions? Deciding to go back to university because you missed out on it in the past? Or is it a vision to open a school in Africa, or a hospital in Asia? Dreams are like a directory of seemingly crazy ideas of what your life can be, and come in the most astounding variety. That enormous crazy dream which terrifies you, that secret ambition you wouldn't dream of telling anyone for fear of looking dumb for even thinking about it - these are the very best kind of dreams anyone can have, because they carry the greatest level of reward and accomplishment.

CHANGE STARTS WITH A DREAM

Elias Howe, who pioneered the modern sewing machine, credited his invention to a dream. Niels Bohr, the Nobel Prize winner, claimed to have seen the structure of the atom in a dream. Indeed, great things happen because of dreams. Dreaming is just as important as breathing and eating. Dreaming big is what brought about some of the greatest achievements of our race. When you have a dream, it means that you can see a different future; a dream gives you a starting point for positive change.

"If you can dream it, you can do it; always remember that this all started with a dream & a mouse!"

- **Walt E. Disney** (American film producer, Animator)

DREAM PIONEERS

"I have a dream that one day this nation will rise up and live out the true meaning of its creed; we hold these truths to be self-evident that all men are created equal... I have a dream that my four little children will one day live in a nation where they will not be judged by the colour of their skin but by the content of their character... I have a dream today."

(Speech at the Civil Rights March on Washington, August 28, 1963)

Of course you will recognise the above excerpt as being from one of the world's most powerful, memorable and quoted speeches in history. It was delivered by one of my heroes; the late Dr. Martin Luther King Jr. Dr. King's dream represented a world free from racial prejudice. He had a vision of equality for all. Dr. King's dream appeared to be highly unrealistic, given the times he was living in. Nonetheless, he dreamed it, believed it, and worked tirelessly to ensure it would happen.

The following people all form the dream pioneers list, because they had the courage to fulfil their dreams. They continue to be positive examples for us to replicate. Walt Disney used his gift of creativity and the power of his imagination to make people smile, laugh, and be happy. Mother Teresa set out to fulfil her mission of caring for the deprived and disadvantaged in society. Mahatma Gandhi's focus was to set his people free from colonial domination. Last, but by no means least, Jesus Christ came to earth to rescue humanity from the power of their sin.

THE EXAMPLE HAS BEEN SET

The Dream Author's Manual says...

"Do you see what this means—all these pioneers who blazed the way, all these veterans cheering us on? It means we had better get on with it. Strip down, start running and never quit! Keep your eyes on Jesus, who both began and finished this race we are in. Study how he did it, because he never lost sight of where he was headed, that exhilarating finish in and with God. He could put up with anything along the way: Cross, shame, whatever, and now he is there, in the place of honour... When you find yourselves flagging in your faith, go over that story again, item by item, that long litany of hostility he ploughed through. That will shoot adrenaline into your souls!"

We have been given the go-ahead to get ahead by a countless list of pioneers. They have set the pace, and it's our duty and privilege to maintain it. Our Dream Pioneers are not only people who have come and gone, but also those who are very much present with us today. They could be directors, actors, sportsmen or entrepreneurs, etc. such as Bill Gates, Tyler Perry, Oprah Winfrey, Michael Jordon, Farrah Gray and Richard Branson. The great news is there is still more than enough space for you on the Dream Pioneers list.

4. HOW FAR DO YOU WANT TO GO?

> *"The person "who walks by faith and not by sense" will have to accept that things don't... work S.M.A.R.T"*

The inspiration for this book came to me as a dream-seed. I remember it was shortly after I attended a life-coaching seminar, where I got talking to a lady with whom I shared my dream. I wanted to write a book about faith, business, and living your dream. That was some years ago. But writing this book has been a life coaching process in itself. There were times when writer's block kicked in and I found no inspiration; I would say "life" took over. Yet this book is in your hands right now just because of my decision to go the distance and see this through to the end. I was spurred on by a key factor that any dream chaser absolutely needs to have.

THE SIXTH SENSE

Most people refer to the "sixth sense" as a gut feeling, instinct, inner voice, or intuition. Whatever you call it, let me tell you that the sixth sense is not just a movie featuring Haley Joel Osment displaying a supernatural power. The sixth sense is what allows ordinary people to do extraordinary things. It is as common and natural as the other five senses that we accept as being valid and real. However, it is unique in that it goes beyond the human intellect.

This additional ability is something called faith. Famous British scientist Sir James Jeans called faith the "sixth sense". He stated, "It enables a person to perceive what lies above and beyond the mere physical and is the sense by which we can understand spiritual matters."

The word 'faith' is often taboo in society because of the negative religious connotations it carries. It brings to mind bible-bashers, religious fanatics, or extremists. Through my own social observations, I have come to understand that our skeptical mind-set is a result of living in a world that trains us that way. Modern education teaches us to accept only what we can determine with our five senses. In fact, it goes a step beyond. It teaches that the only acceptable truth is what has been tried, tested, proved, and approved via scientific methods (experiment, observation, and measurement). However, faith is that priceless ability which empowers us to perceive what lies beyond the limited range of the senses, beyond what our eyes see, our ears hear, our nose smells, our tongue tastes, and our hands feel.

"FAITH is the assurance (the confirmation, the title deed) of the things [we] hope for; being the proof of things [we] do not see and the conviction of their reality. [Faith perceiving as real fact what is not revealed to the senses]

– The Dream Author's Manual

There is yet another sense that is hard at work. This is common sense, which is defined by Merriam-Webster as "sound and prudent judgment based on a simple perception of the situation or facts." Common sense is all about pointing out the seemingly obvious. It is a term used to represent a universally basic level of intelligence that we expect someone to possess. Faith does not always agree with your five senses; they cannot understand its foundation. In the same way, faith often supersedes common sense.

"Faith is believing in something when common sense tells you not to."

From the movie – Miracle On 34th Street"

The person "who walks by faith and not by sense" will have to accept that things don't always work S.M.A.R.T. This will be reiterated as we continue exploring the character of God in relation to this acronym. At the very outset, let me say that any God-given dream you have does not necessarily need to, and will probably not, fit within the context of the S.M.A.R.T. framework or align with its set criteria. You see, this method is man-made while your dream is God-given. Being so, your dream needs more than human theory to make it work.

THE DREAMER'S SUCCESS FORMULA

For big dreamers, there is a simple yet profound formula based on faith. When you do the simple mathematics, it will bring you the life you imagine for yourself.

$$(F+A)=R$$

It you take F (Faith) and add A, it will equal R. It is that straightforward. We can all do this sum regardless of mathematical ability. The rest of the dreamer's success formula will be revealed later on in the book.

There are many who dispute faith and see it as a closed-minded concept. They think that living by faith means living in denial of the realities around them. The truth is, these people are themselves closed-minded. They exhibit the very behaviour they profess to hate. It is the height of ignorance to think that one can live without faith. This attitude shows them to be most certainly out of touch with the reality around them! Regardless of our religious beliefs (or lack of them), we all use faith.

Ernest O'Neill paints a powerful illustration of this in his talk *What is Faith?* O'Neill reminds us that every day we live by faith and that all of us put our faith in some theory or the other. For example, every time you step into a plane (for those that have), you put your faith in the theory of aerodynamics. That faith assures you that this enormous heavy machine weighing thousands of tons will lift into the air, cross thousands of miles of blue sky, and carry you safely to another country.

O'Neill goes on to further say that time after time and in all kinds of situations, we put our faith in people, things, events, techniques, strategies, and in processes that we have not personally tried before, but we trust because of the successful experiences of others in the past. His point is to encourage us that faith is not something strange and superstitious, nor a purely religious or non-rational concept. Instead, it is something that we all practice in our everyday lives.

Science cannot arrive at or prove a definite conclusion about everything that is occurring even in the physical world. For me, faith fills in the gaping holes that science leaves behind. Faith is what gives us a reason to go on despite what our senses tell us. The Dream Author's book gives us an account of someone who, by right, was labelled as the wisest man ever to live. He tried to make sense of the world around him and this was what he had to say...

"I observed all the work of God [and concluded] that man is unable to discover the work that is done under the sun. Even though a man labours hard to explore it, he cannot find it; even if the wise man claims to know it, he is unable to discover it".

– The Dream Author's Manual

In conclusion, stop trying to figure it all out because that will take you a lifetime. Even then, you wouldn't able to make sense of it all. But that's all right because you don't need to understand the work of God; you just need to believe it. Faith is intentional confidence in the character of God.

5. GOD IS NOT SPECIFIC

> *"God often gives us the picture and not the process"*

The S.M.A.R.T. theory insists that your goals, your vision and your dreams be specific. A specific dream is concerned with the details, the intricacies, the 'nitty-gritty' of what you want to achieve. You must be able to clearly express or demonstrate it, leaving nothing implied. In other words, your dream is so clear and to the point that there is no way it can be misunderstood, even by yourself.

According to this theory, a non-specific or vague goal is unlikely to ever be achieved. By being specific, it enters the realm of reality. Having a clear goal will supply answers to every question you have about the steps you need to take towards your dream. However, before you can get answers, you will need to ask questions. They will revolve around these six words:

- Who?
- What?
- Where?
- When?
- Why?
- How?

Here is where the challenge begins. Take a moment to remember your dream. Now ask these six questions, remembering to be as detailed as possible. You will find that you are probably unable to answer all of them. You see, it is impossible to know everything about everything, no matter how hard you try. I suppose if we did, there would never be any problems, you wouldn't be reading this book, and you would already be living your dream. Unfortunately, that is not how it works; we are not perfect and we are not God. But let me tell you, even if you don't know the 'who', 'what' and 'how', it doesn't mean your dream is impossible. All it means is you just don't know everything about it yet. And guess what? That's OK. Just because you don't know everything doesn't mean you should do nothing!

Millions of people have watched their dream shrivel up before their eyes, just because they did not have answers to every question about their dream. They tend to remain stagnant because they couldn't find suitable and/or satisfactory answers, and that drained their confidence to pursue the dream.

To be fair, some people may be able to answer 2, 3, 4 or even all 6 of the questions specifically. But there are ten times as many who don't know the exact details of their dream yet. For them, the S.M.A.R.T. theory has only put their dream farther out of reach.

The problem is that when something seems out of reach, you will never even try to touch it. The dream is, for all practical purposes, a dead object rather than a living, breathing entity. Picture it as a beautiful and immensely useful object that has been stored carefully on the top shelf of your living room. You walk past it every single day without acknowledging it. It hasn't moved or gone anywhere. But you have forgotten it because it is so far above your normal plane of vision.

Over time, it becomes dusty. If, one day, you do notice it, you remember how much you loved it. You feel that you ought to clean it off. It's then that you remember that the reason you left it up there for so long is that you don't have a stepladder to reach so high. The object is like your dream and the stepladder is one of the specifics. You may not have a stepladder to reach your dream but that doesn't mean you can't reach it. Acknowledge your dream, own it, and find another way to achieve it; there is a reason why dust busters were created!

QUESTIONING THE UNKNOWN

"By faith, Abraham obeyed when called to go out to a place that he would receive as an inheritance. Abraham went out not knowing where he was going."

- The Dream Author's Manual

Abraham (formerly called Abram) was given a big dream. In fact, that is an understatement - it was humongous! He was told by God that he would become the father of a great nation, that he would be rich, famous, and be a source of inspiration to many. Let me emphasise this just to make sure you understand how huge this dream was. God's promises to Abraham were these: "Your purpose is to become the founding father of a nation, a world leader. In order to assist your dream so you can make a greater impact, your bank balance will increase. Your name, which is more valuable than money, will carry weight and as a result, you will help millions." That, to me, is mind-blowing stuff. I can only imagine what was going through Abraham's mind at the time and what he would have said, what specific questions he would have asked. If I were to picture what Abraham was thinking at that exact moment, it would have been something like...

"**Who?** Me? **Why** normal, plain ole me? **What** are you talking about? I think you got the wrong person. So **when** is this meant to happen? I'm pretty old, you know. Besides, **where** in the world is this nation? **How** is this even going to be possible?"

DON'T FEAR THE FACTS

> "Faith...allows you to accept a truth without facts"

Abraham probably never took a breath when he fired 101 questions at 101 miles per hour at God. To be honest, if you were given that dream, you'd probably do the same. Correction; maybe you already did get a similar dream and you're asking all the same questions. I bet they are not the ones you always assumed they would be.

When you are working with God-given dreams, you need to understand that God often gives you the picture but not the process (the means to make the dream happen, what will happen, how it will happen, when it will happen, etc.). The reason God often does this is that He knows that if we knew all the specifics, we would probably give up altogether on the dream.

For example, when God gave Joseph a dream, He did not tell him the specifics of all the steps that he would go through. He did not reveal the accusations, temptations, and tribulations right at the start, because he knew Joseph just might have thought twice about embracing that dream. Think about it: if you were told you would become a great leader but first you're going to go to prison, your own family will lie about you and try to kill you (and that's just them!), I know what my normal reaction would be. However, God gave Joseph such a big dream because he knew the stuff Joseph was made of. He knew that boy had what it took to go from stage one to stage two and so forth. The questions Joseph undoubtedly asked found answers only as he walked through his dream journey, and not beforehand. You see, Joseph kept moving forward despite the adversity that he faced. Like Abraham, he was able to do this just by having the picture constantly before him. They did not know the process or the specifics, but they knew God - who was all they needed to go ahead.

"Never give up on what you really want to do. The person with big dreams is more powerful than one with all the facts."

- Unknown

There is power in choosing to possess a big dream. This is the power of faith. It is this faith we talked about earlier, the ability to accept a truth which is more than the sum of the material facts. Faith lets you embrace an idea that could not possibly be true if you went by your intellect alone. Therefore, faith causes you to ignore the normal limiting processes of your mind that say, "I can't", and "I won't". It dismisses your if's and but's. It says, "I can", "I will".

Now therefore, if that's what faith makes you do, isn't it far more positive than giving in to limiting beliefs and self-restricting doubts? Joseph and Abraham decided to act in faith. Despite any fear that may or may not have been present, the gamble paid off, so to speak, because they understood that with God behind your dream, there is no reason why it shouldn't come to amazing fruition.

"God is not a man, that he should lie, nor a son of man, that he should change his mind. Does he speak and then not act? Does he promise and not fulfil?"

- The Dream Author's Manual

This is a rhetorical question. Pure rhetoric, because one of the unique qualities about The Dream Author is that He does not change. He doesn't go back on His word, nor does He have mood swings like us. If He has given you a dream, He does not take it away. There is absolutely no reason God will place a dream seed in your heart and then rip it out by the roots; that's not the way He is, nor does He profit from it. It's YOU who gives it up. You can be assured that if He gave you that dream seed, it will happen - but YOU need to take a step.

Taking a step, just a single step towards your dream, – whether by writing that vision, making that phone call, or sending that letter – makes a statement that says, *"I am in agreement with the dream that You have written for me as the Dream Author of my life and I take this step in recognition of that."*

The all-important and hardest step is always the first one, because it means a choice to leave your old self behind. The journey of a thousand miles has begun, and from then on, everything is going to change radically. You will leave familiarity and comfort for a strange and hard place - but only for a season. This is because though you don't know all that's ahead of you; your pursuit has brought your goal a step nearer.

"Take the first step in faith; you don't have to see the whole staircase, just the first step."

-Martin Luther King Jr (Clergyman, Activist, and Leader)

6. GOD IS NOT MEASURABLE

> *"God the Dream Author is...a gentleman...He wants to work in partnership with you, not against you."*

If you have a measurable goal, you obviously have a set of standards or criteria which you hope to use as way markers towards your dream. These are usually quantifiable. They are supposed to help you stay on track and see how fast you are progressing. It's often said that real objectives are measurable objectives. If it can't be measured, then it can't be achieved.

This looks like a fair assumption. Who wants to lose their way, or veer off course en route to their dream, and risk not achieving it? I certainly don't. However, it is also fair to say there will be times and seasons when you will seem to have gone off track. Even worse, the dream which once enthused you may seem to have developed into a terrible nightmare.

Take it from me that this is an unavoidable situation, no matter how much time you have spent planning. Your reaction, as in any horrible nightmare, is to feel helpless, extremely anxious, and afraid. The dream that glittered before you has become a distant mirage, even farther away today than it was yesterday. You know that feeling when you've done everything humanly possible to make your dream real, but nothing gives? You've taken one step forward repeatedly only to get knocked two steps back. Negative thoughts such as *"I don't think this is going to happen"* start to plague your mind. Discouragement sets in; you feel disheartened, you feel disconnected from your dream, and ultimately, you feel forgotten by The Dream Author.

The fact is, you cannot always measure your progress towards your dream via quantifiable means. Even a S.M.A.R.T. plan doesn't guarantee that things will move according to your calculations. Your markers, criteria, and measurements aren't always suited to a God-given dream. The measuring tape we use is usually flawed; the

Dream Author has a different standard of measurement. After all, His ways and thoughts are not ours, so why would His measurements be?

NO SUCH THING AS A PERFECT PLAN

Have you ever heard the saying "Failure to plan is planning to fail"? It means that lacking a plan of operations, you're probably going to fall flat on your face when it comes to executing your dream. This may be true – but only to an extent. To bring some perspective to that statement, let me point out something important. When you plan, you're preparing ahead of time for a foreseen or predicted task, activity, or event. You plan appropriately to deal with what you expect to happen, much like a shock absorber in a car that cushions the effect of a bad road. But on the flip side, you need a high degree of flexibility in your planning because of the unforeseen. No plan is fail-proof. If you don't recognise this, unexpected roadblocks could just create a bigger shock than your absorbers can handle. Planning does not exempt you from problems; it just prepares you for them.

"The road to success is not straight; there is a curve called failure, a loop called confusion, speed bumps called friends, caution lights called family, and you will have flats called jobs. However, if you have a spare called determination, an engine called perseverance, insurance called faith, and a driver called God, you will make it to a place called success!"

– Unknown

GOD PLANNING OVER GOOD PLANNING

Many people construct Plan A. This is the way they calculate things should be done for the goal to be achieved perfectly. Some create a Plan B just in case Plan A doesn't happen the way they want it to. But if you speak to any successful person who had a plan, you'll notice one outstanding fact. Regardless of how S.M.A.R.T. they were, their dreams were not fully achieved through Plan A or B. Indeed, people with faith acknowledge that neither Plan A nor B is the best or even the first type of plan for a successful dreamer.

Instead, God-planning is the best type of planning you can do. This is simply letting your mind be open and prepared for God. Let Him exert His enormous influence in bringing your dream to life. Why wouldn't you, since He was the One who gave you the dream in the first place? Yet, you wouldn't believe how many people want to exclude Him from the planning process. They think they have it all figured out and want to do things their own way. This huge mistake can turn your dream into a nightmare. You see, God the Dream Author is such a gentleman that He won't take over; He waits for you to welcome his involvement. He wants to work in partnership with you, not against you. The Dream Author's Manual reads...

"Roll your works upon God [commit and trust them wholly to Him; He will cause your thoughts to become agreeable to His will, and] so shall your plans be established *and* succeed."

– The Dream Author's Manual

PRACTICE DOESN'T MAKE PERFECT, IT MAKES IMPROVEMENT

Society says that practice makes perfect – wrong! I once heard Bishop Dale Bronner say, *"...Practice doesn't make perfect, it makes improvement!"* No matter how great your product, service, book, mobile app, phone, or any type of product or service, there will always be a newer and better version of it in a few months or years; this is usually because the first version was not perfect.

When Apple released the first iPad, it wasn't long before they recognised that they could add extra features like a camera. So they went back to the drawing board and came up with the iPad 2 - which was far better. When Twitter adds a feature, they send out an upgrade so members can have smoother service. Many books go through edition after edition to keep up with the new conditions or information that is coming up. Companies review their service parameters and improve where necessary to increase their market share. Did these companies fail to plan the first time around? Was that why their products weren't perfect? Not really. Rather, they know that knowing what improvements can be made comes only with use and practice. Theory is only proven when it's tested.

In the same way, our planning will always be fallible and liable to improvement. What we need, as limited but potentially awesome humans, is to welcome God's total involvement. It really is the best thing even though it may not always seem like it. You see, God has one reason and only one, to object to our plans – if we have strayed off course and are heading in the wrong direction. Just go back to the quotation above, from the Dream Author's book. He says that once you're done planning, give your design to God and let Him take care of it. He is the one who will make your plan successful by adapting, correcting and fine-tuning it. He wants to spare you the pain, unnecessary struggle and preventable resistance that comes from executing a plan outside His agenda.

"Many are the plans in a man's heart, but it is GOD's purpose that prevails."

- The Dream Author's Manual

THE HEART OF THE MATTER IS A MATTER OF THE HEART

"God is not measurable, it is particularly important to know God does measure us"

Coming to ideas, we people can be really wishy-washy sometimes. Today's good idea may be tomorrow's trash. This is precisely the point why we need to allow God to take the wheel of our dream and steer us in the right direction.

This starts from the beginning. What is the root of your dream? Is it God-birthed or born of your bitterness or selfish ambitions? If it's not of God, it doesn't matter how carefully you plan, or how thoroughly you orchestrate its working; when it comes down to it you will always be moving to an awkward rhythm.

Knowing that God is not measurable, it is particularly important to know God does measure us. God's unchangeable standard of measurement has always been different from ours. While some of us are trying to look the part, God examines the heart, from where character flows. While we measure our progress by quantifiable means, God evaluates our growth towards our dream in terms of the quality of our lives.

"God 'measures' a person differently than humans do. Men and women look at appearances, God looks into the heart."

– The Dream Author's Manual

The heart is the centre of your total personality. It determines your intuition, emotions, and feelings; it forms your total character. In contrast, the head is the centre of human intellect. To pursue your big dream successfully, you need heart, not just head. To have heart is to have spirit, courage, enthusiasm and most importantly character. These are some of the key ingredients needed to transform your dream into a masterpiece.

"Character is higher than intellect. A great soul will be strong to live as well as think."

- Ralph Waldo Emerson (American essayist, Lecturer, & Poet)

I hope you've got it by now. This book is not about improving your intelligence. Rather, it focuses on what is deep down inside your heart. I want to address that overwhelming longing and pull which doesn't seem "intelligent" to others - or even to you!

"The human heart feels things the eyes cannot see, and knows what the mind cannot understand."

- Robert Valett (Author)

Joseph was a young man with heart. He experienced one cruel setback after another, sinking as low as you could possibly imagine, and all because he possessed a big dream. If he had measured his progress quantifiably, he certainly would have considered it time to give up and just given in! However, he stepped up and stepped out, using every obstacle as a stepping-stone, to show heart. I gave you just a snippet of this stimulating biography earlier. But if you've never heard of him before, I suggest you pick up the Dream Author's Manual and be inspired. God is too big as well as too marvellous to fathom, so without doubt it is impossible for us to measure His wisdom and foresight. You will cry out at times, "God, what are you doing?" in your frustration with the unknown and unforeseeable, but as a dreamer it's not the absence of obstacles that reassures you as to your progress. Rather, it is the conviction of God's purpose for you, which empowers you to have the heart to proceed forward.

"The size of your success is measured by the strength of your desire, the size of your dream, and how you handle disappointment along the way."

- **Robert Kiyosaki** (American investor, Businessman, Author)

And there are many others who had 'heart'. Chris Gardner, the father whose life journey was superbly depicted by actor Will Smith in the film the 'Pursuit of Happyness', is another example. His life story inspires me and brings me to tears because there were points in his life when it seemed like there was no progress at all. Nevertheless, he had a driving passion in his heart. He knew he had to change his life, not just for himself but for his son. With this dream, and despite his setbacks, he kept pressing on.

"I was homeless, but I wasn't hopeless. I knew a better day was coming."

- **Chris Gardner** (American Entrepreneur, Investor, Author)

7. GOD IS NOT ATTAINABLE

> *God doesn't care if you are black, white, or purple, if you are rich or poor, tall or short. He knows exactly where you are at...you just need to stop making excuses.*

Is your dream attainable? When you answer that in the affirmative, you say it is capable of being accomplished, achieved or obtained. It means you are certain that given your current situation, resources and available time, there's a good chance of a favourable outcome. But if you don't have that degree of confidence, your foundation is weak. Attaining your dream is not quite feasible. So, at least, goes the S.M.A.R.T teaching.

But if you take a good hard look at the size of your dream, what it really means, and then compare it with your current reality, you may more often than not start to realise that you and your dream are worlds apart. In all probability, your dream looks unattainable, given your present life circumstances, your lack of knowledge and/or skill, inexperience, lack of enough resources to facilitate the dream (computers, tools, money, etc.), or not having direct access to key people, mentors, etc.

The real issue arises when you are faced with a huge, apparently unbridgeable gap between your current reality and future aspirations. What do you do then? Do you wander around there, staring at the gap? Do you start feeling a sense of emptiness, knowing in your heart that something vital is missing from that picture – but never realising that the missing piece is you? The more time you spend doing nothing about bridging that gap, the more time passes in emptiness. The bigger that gap grows, the greater the distance separating you from your dream. The more likely it is that you will fill that void with unfruitful and unproductive activity instead of throwing yourself across the gap.

DREAM DRAINS

Let's stop throwing excuses at the inner emptiness. The word "excuse" has many definitions. I have a combined version: "An excuse is an explanation given in the attempt to exonerate oneself from the responsibility of doing his or her duty."

Excuses are a waste of time, given to justify our failure to do what we know we should have done, or should be doing but aren't. Excuses just mean you're giving up or giving in to fear, ignorance or laziness. I truly feel that when you give up, it only means you can't be bothered. You didn't explore all your options; instead, you ignored or denied them. You didn't plan ahead or go ahead. You didn't humbly ask for help when it was needed; or you disregarded offered help. In such a situation, an excuse is sheer dishonesty. You are deceiving yourself even more than others.

I call excuses 'Dream Drains'. Once you start down that path, it is exactly where your dream goes, down the drain, which makes that glugging sound as it slowly sucks and swallows every ounce of your longing, leaving you dry and empty. One drain is probably working right now - your inner sceptic and/or your negative external voice which keeps saying, *"You know that this really doesn't make any difference; your dream will not happen; God is not SMART is just another one of those books"*.

When this happens, our first and greatest mistake is to agree. Instead of dismissing the excuse on the spot, we dally with it. Very quickly, it begins to invade your thoughts and then to preen openly. How you think does determine the way you act. If you see an obstacle rather than a stepping-stone in every circumstance, you will shrink from opportunity. You will create excuses for not going ahead with your dream. Finally, your excuses will take on a life of their own, birthing negative confessions.

Let's look at some familiar and common Dream Drains below:

The Socioeconomic Dream Drain: "My circumstances are just not up to it (based upon how much we have available). I don't have a first-class degree; I graduated from a small college; my job is too humble."

The Geographical Dream Drain: "My location just isn't right. Newcastle isn't New York. I don't have opportunity." The truth is that extra opportunities do produce extra challenges, which demand extra changes; but there's nowhere you can't grow a dream.

The Time Dream Drain: "I don't have time to work on it; it takes too long. I can't do it today; there is always tomorrow." Well, there's so much to say about this that I'll leave it for chapter 9
.
The Credibility Dream Drain: "I'm not smart, qualified, special or significant enough to work out such a big dream."

The Relationship Dream Drain: "My surroundings don't allow me to pursue my dream. My social circle is incompatible with it. I don't know what people will say. My family and friends would never understand." We also carry emotional baggage from the past. "He/she hurt me badly and now I'm afraid."

The Ethnicity, Gender & Age Dream Drain: "I'm not that kind. My makeup just isn't that way. I'm a man/woman. I'm too young/ too old for this. My parents expect something different." You see, your birth culture and ethnicity, your gender and age, all show up in the way you think, the aspirations you personally cherish. But that isn't God's way.

The Fear Dream Drain: This umbrella term sums up all of the above. Fear is the direct opposite of faith. It is a disruptive and unsettling force, which can be hard to shake off once you've been living with it for some time. It makes you act and react negatively; always seeing threats everywhere, real or imaginary.

THERE IS NO GOOD REASON FOR YOUR LAME EXCUSE

These excuses may be genuine reasons for limitations or just a lame excuses. But wait! There is a way to tell the difference.

You know what an excuse is. Now a reason is an explanation given for why something is the way it is. The difference is when you give a reason you take responsibility for your part in the situation or outcome. However, an excuse is just disclaiming your responsibility to live the life you were intended to live. You put the blame on everything and everyone around instead. Now why would you lie to yourself like that?

Without discounting your life experiences, your disabilities and handicaps, your tragedies and poverty, I still need to ask you, have you done all you could and should to put substance into your dream? Or is your dream glugging slowly down the drain while you watch?

"If you really want to do something, you'll find a way; if you don't, you'll find an excuse."

– Frank Banks (American Actor)

Moses was a great leader of his people. But when the Dream Author gave him his impossible dream, he made excuses. He reacted as anyone would, with major doubts, because of what he thought was his weak starting position. His conversation with God was something like this:

"Ummm, God, **who am I** that I should go to Pharaoh, and that I should bring the children of Israel out of Egypt. I'm just an old man with a rod, and **what if** they don't believe me? **Why** would they believe me? I mean, **how** am I going to speak to these people? I am not eloquent. And, to top it all, I stammer!"

Moses listed most of his weaknesses, all of his fears and doubts. But it seems like he left out something. He didn't list his amnesia! You see, Moses had forgotten who gave him that vision. Moses had forgotten that God doesn't care if you are black, white, or purple, if you are rich or poor, tall or short. He knows exactly where you are at, and He knows what you are called to be. God does not call the qualified, but he qualifies the called; you just need to stop making excuses and get with the programme.

STRETCH YOURSELF

In fact, it is your supposed weakness at the start that really develops and stretches you. At journey's end, you will notice with gratitude that the run developed muscle out of all the flab you carried when you started out. If you knew nothing about business before you started your company, at the finish you will have learned invaluable lessons about doing business that only experience can teach – whether your company survives or not. I remember a quote that said *'There is no failure in feedback'*, and that is exactly the attitude to challenges that we need to adopt. Thomas Edison, who made the first practical light bulb, is famously supposed to have said, *"If I find 10,000 ways something won't work, I haven't failed. I am not discouraged because every wrong attempt discarded is another step forward"*.

Coming back to Moses, the only resource he had to realise his dream was his rod. But while he was debating with God about his call, about all he *didn't* have, he was completely ignoring and devaluing what he did have. But God would have none of it! He showed Moses the power in his hands. What He instructed Moses to do was to "...Stretch out your hand and *grasp it!* ..."

Moses had to stretch, reach forward, and grab. Until he did that, he would never have realised the power that was at work within him, the strength available to him. Just so, you need to stretch if you are to seize your tool and use it. All of us have rods, overlooked skills and abilities that we use on a daily basis. The truth is we can have a million excuses not to use them, but if you have just one good reason to do it, that will be all you need.

56

8. GOD IS NOT REALISTIC

> *God-given dreams rarely seem realistic... if a dream is from God...it is often 'bigger' than you*

To be 'Realistic' is to 'interested in, concerned with, or based upon what is real and/or practical'. As far as the S.M.A.R.T. acronym goes, 'realistic' is the sum total of the first three acronyms because a dream that is specific, measurable, and attainable, will be realistic. However, being realistic goes much further. It defines whether the dream is one that was even possible to begin with.

The problem with the S.M.A.R.T. theory is that it weeds out a whole lot of people at the very start. These are the guys who, right at the onset, are not sure how to specify their dream, set up indicators for their progress and break it down into attainable steps. They don't know how to nurture and nourish the dream seed that was planted by using this plan. Their dream is so big that S.M.A.R.T. labels it as 'unrealistic' and out of reach.

But don't worry. God-given dreams rarely seem realistic. In fact, one common way to know if a dream is from God is that it is often 'bigger' than you. Pursuing it will require some stretching. It is a mistake to live only by your five natural senses; you risk limiting yourself severely. But if you add the faculty of faith, using your sixth sense, life becomes full of boundless possibilities. Where we go wrong is the fact that we assume we know what will happen if we try out something. This kind of risk calculation based on 'reasonable' assumptions constricts life. How can you say something is impossible without trying it?

"...With men it is impossible, but not with God; for with God all things are possible."

- The Dream Author's Manual

You need to know that the secret to attaining your dream is based on the Dream Author; it doesn't depend on whether it looks or is realistic. The required difference, the magical transformation, the single apostrophe that turns 'Impossible' into 'I'm possible' – is the Dream Author himself. So never rule out anything just because it's unrealistic. Anything is possible if it's based on Him – whether it's practical or not.

"Plans have to be realistic; dreams don't."

- Richard Templar (British Author)

Let me go out on a limb here. I dare to say that if you're the kind who plans first and then starts to believe you can do it, you don't have the kind of faith you need to make your dream come true. You have a 'scientific faith', which means you only believe it if you can prove it. While I don't discourage planning, I want to make it clear that plans are just that – they are not dreams. You need to believe in your dream and its Author even before you start planning. You need to start planning because you believe in your dream.

"Without leaps of imagination, or dreaming, we lose the excitement of possibilities. Dreaming, after all, is a form of planning."

– **Gloria Steinem** (American feminist, Journalist, Activist)

STATISTICS ARE NOT FIXED

Inspiration to make your dream a solid reality is found everywhere. We read and hear stories every day of people who made unrealistic dreams a reality. Let me fan your faith with a quick synopsis of some of these people.

Richard Branson, One of the top 25 richest people in the UK according to the 26th annual Sunday Times Rich List 2014, was dyslexic, labelled an academic failure and a school dropout. Defying the assumptions of his teachers and other experts, he overcome his realistic conditions, beating the odds stacked against him, by starting a small record store to now experiencing success in a range of highly profitable ventures from mobile phones to airlines.

Stevie Wonder, an iconic musician who has been blind from birth, beautifully plays the piano and writes songs without ever seeing a pen or paper. He is a celebrated example of someone who has done the impossible. The 22 Grammy awards he has won over his 51 plus year music career demonstrates that he conquered his "reality" to realise his dreams.

J.K. Rowling was a divorced single mother struggling on benefits/welfare. The first draft of *Harry Potter and the Philosopher's Stone* was rejected by most leading publishers. She conquered her "reality" by persistently continuing to submit it her book until someone finally decided to take a chance. Her books turned movies have topped the charts ever since.

Susan Boyle (Britains Got Talent Winner, 2009), at the age of 48, was a church singer. She lived quietly, looking after her mother, and was somewhat of a stranger to the community. She had a dream of being a famous singer, a dream she held onto for many years. After a decision to go on 'Britain's Got Talent', she was immediately judged on her appearance and eccentric personality. Susan conquered her "reality" Once she revealed her gift, she silenced the world and went on to become one of the fastest-selling debut artists of all time.

Hellen Keller was deaf and blind, because of a severe fever contracted in infancy. Yet she had a dream to live a normal life. Helen conquered her "reality" and went on to become the first deaf and blind person to earn a Bachelor of Arts degree, as well as an Author, Political activist, and Lecturer.

These are just a few examples of what happens if you have a vision of what your life should be, and don't allow your supposed disabilities to hinder it.

"The only thing worse in the world than being blind is to have sight but no vision."

– Helen Keller

I admire the metamorphosis of Stan 'Tookie' Williams who was a founding member of the infamous 'Crips', a notorious street gang started in South Central Los Angeles in 1969. Ten years later (1979), he was convicted of four murders committed in the course of robberies, and sentenced to death. However, while in prison, he made a complete U-turn. Renouncing his gang affiliation, he expressed remorse for having founded the Crips. He wrote and spoke against gang activity in several books. This unlikely author eventually produced anti-gang, anti-violence and children's literature. He was nominated for the Noble Prize for Peace, usually reserved for intellectuals, devout and pious people or prestigious figures! Was this a realistic destiny for a gangster, thug and a murderer? Yet it really happened.

A great many unrealistic things happen every day. The reason they proved to be possible is that someone dared to dream big, and did not allow a statistic or probability to define them. Practically speaking, these people should not have been able to accomplish what they did, but somehow they hung on through sheer grit and determination, proving you can do it!

It doesn't matter what your teachers, parents, friends or colleagues thought of you. It doesn't matter what facts are quoted, or which statistics are marshalled against you. These are earth-bound and they can change. People have proved over and over again that faith overrides facts. No one can minimise your dream with S.M.A.R.T. talk. If anyone tries, don't humour him or her, but conscientiously dismiss their "realism"

"The difference between a stumbling block and a stepping stone is how high you raise your foot."

– **Benny Lewis** (Author)

9. GOD IS NOT TIME-BOUND

To be time-bound requires you to set a period for taking each step toward your goal, or to set deadlines to accomplish the final target. In our case, we are talking about your dream. S.M.A.R.T. means you have to set a day, month, and year when you will achieve your dream.

> *"...a process of preparation, ploughing and patience...God uses to build and qualify us for our destiny."*

The time-bound execution of your dream can only take place if you have achieved the other four steps. You cannot plan or create a time frame without a specific goal. Knowing what you want to do is crucial to creating a time-bound plan. This step is meant to increase the level of motivation and the urgency required to complete all necessary actions within the time constraint.

Does this apply to a God-given dream? What I want to know is how many times you have set up this kind of timeline for your dream, and the date has come and gone? I guess it has happened to you many times. The reason is that life, with all its unexpected twists and turns, difficulties and challenges, stepped in to throw your S.M.A.R.T time plan out of joint. Very often we underestimate all that is required to make our dream work.

What I have learned is that setting inappropriate time scales finally results in your dream being shelved. In contrast, a God-given dream requires firstly that we accept a different time-scale. God-time is not our time. Time is not relevant to God the same way it is to us.

"Do not let this one fact escape you... with God one day is as a thousand years and a thousand years as one day."

– The Dream Author's Manual

Secondly, time is an ever-flowing stream. It doesn't stop to let you pick yourself up and start over because you lost control of your time. Correction: you never did control your time. All you could ever do was control the way you used it. You and everyone else have the responsibility to manage the 24 hours we get each day, to pursue your purpose productively. But when you use words like 'time-bound', 'constraints' and 'deadline', you brand time negatively in connection with your dream. This is a huge contradiction. When the Dream Author who gave you your dream is beyond time, does it make sense that your dream is time-bound and constrained?

Yet we know that God created time for us, though He is not limited by it Himself. God does everything for a purpose. If time serves a purpose, then what is this purpose?

TIME TO GROW UP!

"God gives us dreams a size too big so that we can grow into them."

- Unknown

The purpose of time is growth. Growth is an essential process. It takes time. Growth is the process of developing physically, mentally, and spiritually. It is the process of growing organically from one stage to the next, changing and refining and becoming greater, larger, and more substantial. Growth is all a matter of increase.

We all reach dream maturity through a process of preparation, ploughing and patience, which God uses to build and qualify us for our destiny. The time of moulding and pressing ensures that we will fully appreciate and safeguard the splendour of full fruition. If our dream came about without effort and toil, we would abuse it, and it would destroy us. For example, some people are destroyed by winning a lottery and gaining wealth beyond their wildest dreams. Since they never went through the discipline of honest toil and effort to gain riches, they have no financial intelligence. They spend a fortune on frivolity and self-indulgence, and it finally leads them astray. This immaturity is the trademark of anyone who attempts to taste the fruit of success without putting down the roots of effort. What they enjoy has not been "rightfully" won, and so they don't value it as they should.

God typically gives you the picture and not the process, when it comes to your dream, because He requires you to grow. If most of us were to see all the blood, sweat, and tears that go into making a dream happen, we would shrink from the challenge. But there are no shortcuts to a real dream. Shortcuts tend to cut short the vital root-shoot-fruit growth that needs to take place within the individual. Therefore, if you want to enjoy your dream, you'll need to learn to endure for your dream. Allow yourself the process of time, and don't be hasty. You can't plant an apple tree today and expect to eat apple pie tomorrow.

"The fruit of your labour will yield after the process has taken place."

- **The Dream Author's Manual**

THE PROCESS OF TIME

There is an appointed time for the full manifestation of your dream. Being so splendid and unique, your dream deserves time to mature and become magnificent reality. Since things rarely go according to plan, we need to change the way we look at time. Time is a resource that is indispensable in the process of realising your dream.

"Life is all about timing... the unreachable becomes reachable, the unavailable become available, the unattainable... attainable. Have the patience, wait it out. It's all about timing."

- **Stacey Charter** (Cancer Survivor)

It's all about the timing, seasons, appointed moments in which things will happen. As The Dream Author's manual says:

"To everything there is a season, a time for every purpose under heaven: a time to be born, and a time to die; a time to plant, and a time to pluck what is planted; a time to kill, and a time to heal; a time to break down, and a time to build up; a time to weep, and a time to laugh; a time to mourn, and a time to dance; a time to cast away stones, and a time to gather stones; a time to

embrace, and a time to refrain from embracing; a time to gain, and a time to lose; a time to keep, and a time to throw away; a time to tear, and a time to sew; a time to keep silence, and a time to speak; a time to love, and a time to hate; a time of war, and a time of peace."

– The Dream Author's manual

This related quotation strikes another note on the value of time in relation to achieving our dreams.

'TAKE TIME'

"Take time to think - it is the source of all power.
Take time to read - it is the fountain of wisdom.
Take time to play -it is the source of perpetual youth.
Take time to be quiet - it is the opportunity to seek God.
Take time to be aware - it is the opportunity to help others.
Take time to love and be loved - it is God's greatest gift.
Take time to laugh - it is the music of the soul.
Take time to be friendly - it is the road to happiness.
Take time to dream - it is what the future is made of.
Take time to pray - it is the greatest power on earth.
Take time to give - it is too short a day to be selfish.
Take time to work - it is the price of success.

There is a time for everything."

- Author Unknown

The Dream Author's vision will certainly come true in your future. You will attain your dream. But the time frame is not within your control. It may take longer than you think.

"At the time I have decided, my words will come true. You can trust what I say about the future. It may take a long time, but keep on waiting - it will happen!"

- The Dream Author's Manual

Although we all want our dreams to happen as soon as possible, we are encouraged by God to be patient and to hold on! Waiting is not procrastinating. Waiting expectantly is to hold on to the promise and the vision you have received, while procrastination is being your own worst enemy by not doing your part when you need to. I personally do not advocate or condone the idea that your dream will "just" happen when it's ready; rather my point here is to emphasise that your dream may not happen overnight, but it will happen as long as you believe it, and act on your belief. As Neal A. Maxwell said, 'Faith in God also means faith in His timing.'

10. GOD IS NOT S.M.A.R.T., GOD IS WISE!

God may not be the "S.M.A.R.T.-est" person, but God most certainly is the wisest. God knows everything, God is the one who has all the facts whose insight cannot be paralleled. He is more powerful than google and yields results which are more credible. Theologians call this character trait "omniscient" which means 'All Knowing'. In addition, God's wisdom is not just a matter of knowledge, but "know how." God's wisdom means He knows how to do anything, which is especially important as we previously explored, as this means we can rely upon His direction.

It is for this reason that He is known as "the only wise God". Wisdom is rooted in God's essential character; He is the epitome of Wisdom. It is made evident in His doing the best thing, in the best way, at the best time and for the best purpose. God's wisdom defies social convention. God will not be **S**pecific, **M**easurable, **A**ttainable, **R**ealistic and **T**ime-bound because S.M.A.R.T. is only fitting from a human perspective. It is impossible to over-emphasise this point. Let me conclude by reiterating that it is important to accept that God knows what He is doing, even if you don't.

"Trust God from the bottom of your heart; don't try to figure out everything on your own. Listen for God's voice in everything you do, everywhere you go; He's the one who will keep you on track. Don't assume that you know it all."

- The Dream Author's Manual

PART TWO: GET UP, GET GOING & GET AHEAD - COACHING YOU TO YOUR DREAMS

11. THE DREAM COACH

Welcome to part two of God Is Not S.M.A.R.T. So far, we have gained some insight about the character of God and why He does what He does, with the dream He gave you. Nonetheless, it only makes sense that I use the rest of the book to deal with the heart of the matter...you! In fact, this book really has been all about you. I want to get you to realise your potential, your purpose and live your passion. I am trying to get you to the place where you won't think, "If it happens", but "I'm going to make it happen."

No matter how much passion and conviction I put into my words, I cannot make you do anything you don't want to. As they say, "You can lead a horse to the water but you can't force it to drink." Remember, I am presenting you with new options, a different perspective on life. Ask yourself the question: "Why can't I live life to the fullest?" It all comes down to choice. That's really the only major difference between you and any celebrity, millionaire, or successful professional.

From now on, I am your Dream Coach. I am offering you down-to-earth advice that will give you the grip on attaining your dreams. I want to highlight some key areas you should be conscious of, and some useful tips to apply at any stage of your dream journey.

WHAT IS COACHING?

Most people visualise a coach as a man yelling from the side-lines, telling his players what to do, instructing and motivating them so that they can win. He is critically involved in their play though he is not directly playing on the field. The coach plays a vital role in the peak performance of his athletes. The coach may not be a star player himself but his skill lies in being able to bring out the best in his protégé. For example, Usain Bolt, the fastest man on the earth, has a coach. The coach cannot run as fast as Bolt. What he offers is something different – the motivation and skills to be the fastest and hold on to that title.

Similarly, life coaching is all about assisting an individual to reach his or her goal by building up their skills and transforming mind-sets. Coaching is about getting results, which is the sum total of the Dreamer's Success Formula. (**Faith** + **A**) = **R**ESULTS.

But getting the results you want requires giving it all you've got. I will be your coach, even though I am by no means an Olympic athlete. I can still most definitely yell at you from the side-lines with my mantra, *"Get up, get going, and GET AHEAD!"*

12. ARISE AND SHINE

WAKE UP

Remember when your mother would try to get you up in the morning for school? She would disrupt your comfortable slumber, routing you out of your warm cosy bed and shouting, *"Wakey, wakey, arise and shine!"* Who knew these words actually carried great meaning?

"Arise; get out of bed; wake up! |Don't stay in the comfort of your circumstances, arise to a new life and shine bright."

– The Dream Author's Manual

To understand the significance of the words 'wake up', apart from the obvious, there are a couple of definitions of the word "wake' that struck me:

- To become roused from a tranquil or inactive state; awaken; waken: to wake from one's daydreams.

- To become cognizant or aware of something; awaken; waken: to wake to the true situation.

- To remain awake for some purpose, duty, etc.

As I looked at these definitions, a thought came to my mind. Many people are sleep walking, unaware that physically they are on the move but mentally and even spiritually they are still very much asleep. This is dangerous! To be mentally motionless and spiritually inactive will cause one to press the snooze button of life one too many times. From the comfort of your bed, nothing will change and the pleasure of sleep will not turn things around even if you are dreaming big dreams. The reason why you wake is that you realise there is a purpose to get up to, a gift that should be kindled to fervency. And you rise because every hour you sleep is an extra hour you'll never get back.

"If you want to make your dreams come true, the first thing you have to do is wake up."

- **J.M Power** (Writer)

Waking up is that moment of realisation, the instant when unreality fades away and things begin to take on a different, sharper meaning. Finally, you understand what life is about. Your perspective is changing for the better. You've realised that God is not S.M.A.R.T., so why should you be?

"The best way to make your dreams come true is to wake up."

- **Paul Valery** (French poet, Essayist, and Philosopher)

PAY ATTENTION

There is a line in a song from one of my favourite movies - *Sister*, Act 2, which goes:

"If you wanna be somebody, if you wanna go somewhere, you better **wake up** *and* **pay attention.***"*

Simple but powerful. This instruction is serious. You are to wake up and pay attention. Waking up is not enough; you have to pay attention. You need to be alert, aware, and receptive. If you pay attention to something, you take notice; you concentrate on it; it becomes your focus. This is the crucial difference between being awake, and paying attention.

"I think the one lesson I have learned is that there is no substitute for paying attention."

– **Diane Sawyer** (News Anchor)

Another aspect of paying attention to your dream is that there is a cost involved; it isn't a free ride. A friend once said to me, *"Anthony, a pioneer paves the way; but they also pay the way!"* Every pioneer and dreamer, including those mentioned above, including you, has paid the full cost of realising their dreams. The currency you pay with is your complete attention. Only 100% will do. There is no place for half-hearted attempts. Give it your best; a man can give nothing more.

A major truth you need to know is that while your wings are sprouting, and you're paying attention to your dream, many people around you will dismiss you as foolish and impractical. There won't be anybody around when you need support. Bill Gates experienced this while he was on the brink of one of the biggest breakthroughs with Microsoft. Some saw his ideas as foolish and chose not to "pay attention". They missed out massively on the profits that came when Microsoft was launched. One major lesson I have learned is: "Before you make it, people will not pay you any attention; but after you make it, people will pay for your attention."

"Paying attention to simple little things that most men neglect makes a few men rich."

- **Henry Ford** (American Industrialist)

13. LIGHTS, CAMERA, ACTION!

How FAR are you willing to go? The distance hugely depends on adding F and A together, and A is the missing factor to complete the dreamer's success formula.

Action (A) is what you need to add to your F to continue your dream journey. Observe the updated formula (**Faith** + **Action**) = **Results**. To prove that you've made up your mind about turning your life around and living purposefully, let your actions support your faith. As a popular text from the Dream Author's manual says, *"Faith without ACTION is dead";* it is lifeless, useless, and worthless: it is a subtraction when your focus should be addition. This truth may be a hard pill to swallow. But there's no way I'm going to give you all the faith talk and finish up, right?

ACTION PROVES DECISION

You have made a choice to wake up and pay attention, which in itself is an action, but don't be under any illusion that that was it. That doesn't cut any ice. If you did, shame on you! Do you think Martin Luther King Jr. or Mother Teresa sat down saying "God is Not S.M.A.R.T., so I'll just wait on him"? No way! They understood that because God is Not S.M.A.R.T, they don't have to be held back by their limitations. They realised that the only thing which could prevent them from attaining their dream was themselves. This stirred them up to act in accordance to their belief.

"Remember, a real decision is measured by the fact that you've taken new action. If there is no action, you haven't truly decided."

- Tony Robbins (Self-help author and motivational speaker)

God Is Not S.M.A.R.T is all about changing and challenging popular mind-sets, attitudes and schools of thought, including your approach to your life and your dream. It really doesn't matter how "smart" you are. What truly determines if you are intelligent is applied action.

"Action is the real measure of intelligence."

- **Napoleon Hill** (American Author)

It doesn't even matter how educated or up-to-date you are with the latest planning, management and business theories, hypotheses and all the other big words - because that is all just knowledge. It means nothing without implementation. Achieving your dream is not about what you know, but what you do.

"An ounce of action is worth a ton of theory."

- **Ralph Waldo Emerson** (American essayist, Lecturer, and Poet)

14.   WATCH YOUR ASS!

"Watch your thoughts; they become words. Watch your words; they become actions. Watch your actions; they become habit. Watch your habits; they become character. Watch your character; it becomes your destiny."

- Unknown

While you are watching your thoughts, words, actions, habits and character, you also need to keep an eye on what's going on out back. Go on, turn around, look and take notice of what you see. It should be really noticeable, hard to overlook and easily identifiable. Can you see it?

Well ...what you should see is your ass! Americans say it all the time, *"You better watch your ass!"* In truth, that is a great piece of advice, especially if you have a big dream and have started to take action. But (pun intended), you need to assess the ass you got behind you because it can either make your dream or break your dream - if you don't watch out. There are two types of ass to look out for:

DREAM ASS-ASSINS

Dream Assassins are those people in your life whose sole purpose seems to be to steal, kill and ultimately destroy your dream. These people are usually insecure; they feel threatened by you, your life, your dream, and your dazzling potential. Their envy causes them to react negatively.

A quote by Harold Coffin says, *"Envy is the art of counting others' blessings instead of your own"*. People who devote their time to assassinating you don't know who they are or what their purpose is. They are jealous, angry, and frustrated. Without a dream of their own, they can only look at what you have and try to destroy it.

An assassination is a deliberate attack on a person, usually a prominent figure, often for political reasons. The motives could be religious, ideological or political. Other times, it may be for financial gain, revenge for perceived grievances, or from a desire for fame or notoriety.

Two great examples of unsuccessful assassination attempts are that of Dr. Martin Luther King Jr and the Biblical figure, Joseph. Dr. King's life was cut short when he was assassinated on 4th April, 1968, in the southern US city of Memphis, Tennessee. He was just 39. Yet, I smile as I write this, not because of the tragedy of his death but because 46 years later, Dr. King's dream is still living and active. His dream is coming alive through the medium of world-changers like you and me. So yes, I meant it when I described it as an unsuccessful assassination.

Assassins don't always kill your body; it's often easier and more effective to destroy and tarnish your character and integrity. Dream assassins use any and every opportunity they have to do this. They have a variety of methods to fulfil their destructive mission. One of the most popular methods is to create a rumour, and attach your name to it.

"RUMOR: A favourite weapon of the assassins of character."

- Ambrose Bierce (American Editorialist, Journalist)

Rumours are gossip, hearsay. They are stories which circulate without certainty or confirmation of facts, pretty much like a BlackBerry Messenger broadcast message. 'Word of mouth' is a perennial success in rumour-spreading. The most high-budget advertising can't buy the level of exposure you have when folks gossip to each other. And most people are so gullible they believe all they hear. This is why our media make rich profits.

How can you defend yourself? A word to the wise: there is minimal room for rumours to live if your life is exemplary, like Joseph and Mr. King. Don't give dream assassins an opportunity by questionable words or deeds.

Assassins devote much thought to the death of your dream. They plan it, they train for it, and they study you to find out your weakest spot. You need to realise how driven they are. Your failure means so much to them. This is why they strategise so deeply and why they rarely act on impulse. The risk is too great; they cannot afford to fail because they only have one shot. If it doesn't work or if it backfires, they lose everything. Not only are they exposed for who they really are, but they remain losers themselves.

I tell you all this because you need to be aware of these voices of pessimism and negativity that verbally assassinate your dream. You need to avoid those kill-joys who always see every half-full glass as half-empty, the kind who scoff at the idea of a silver lining in any cloud, who always predict rain on your parade (and bring it too!). You need to avoid them like the Ebola virus, because of the subtle way in which they kill your dream. They start by dropping, knowingly or unknowingly, one small negative word that may or may not be noticed. Then they multiply their verbal stabs, and the infection multiplies. These words destroy anything they attach to. This is not science fiction but a dreadful reality. These people corrupt moral standards, intellect and beliefs. You should never share your dream with them, no matter how carried away you are. They will puncture your balloon and send you crashing down to earth from the delightful heights of your dream utopia. These are the S.M.A.R.T people. They call themselves realists because they take it on themselves to remind you of the unfavourable reality of your present circumstances. In fact, they do not know or appreciate the significance and the certainty of hope, the importance of aspirations and of running with a God-given life dream.

So much for assassins from outside. But what about self-assassination, when you try to kill your own dream? You do this, consciously or unconsciously, when you embrace habits like:

- Self-limiting beliefs – the dark clouds of pessimism and unbelief which hover over our lives because we ourselves put them there.

- Procrastination and laziness – the attitude that it's always better to start working on your dream tomorrow, because today suffers from many limitations – as you have already read!

"Procrastination is opportunity's natural assassin."

- **Victor Kiam** (Entrepreneur)

DREAM ASS-ISTANTS

"No matter what accomplishments you make, somebody helped you."

– **Althea Gibson** (American Tennis Player)

A Dream Assistant is a person who helps you with a need, or pushes toward the achievement of a goal, a purpose or an effort, regarding your dream. They are always backing you up, supporting your vision, and investing time, talents and even money ungrudgingly to see it come true. They are devoted to helping you. We all need them. No man is an island, and we all need help from others. There is no shame in asking for help when we cannot do something. The shame is in leaving it undone because we were too proud to ask for help.

"What separates those who achieve from those who don't is in direct proportion to one's ability to ask for help."

– Unknown

Obviously, you have neither the resources nor the accomplishments to make your dream a reality by yourself. We know this already since we discussed this in chapter 11 - God is not Attainable. This is why God sends you dream assistants. They are part of that crucial link between you and your dream. Moses, the man with a million excuses, needed an assistant to aid him in his pursuit of his dream (purpose). He got a man called Joshua. Joshua was a courageous individual who stood out without flinching, because he knew that sometimes you need to stand out to be outstanding. He was willing to stake all he had to help fulfil the calling of Moses.

"... **Joshua the son of Nun, Moses' assistant,** *one* **of his choice men...**"

- The Dream Author's Manual

Once you focus on your dream, you will come to understand that every Moses needs a Joshua. Everyone with a dream needs someone to stand with them and support them.

As we look on, we see Moses leaning heavily on Joshua at some pivotal moments of his life. With Joshua at his side, Moses went up - not down or away. Without his help, Moses might not have done some of those marvellous things he was privileged to do. The accounts and historical moments we cherish today would have lacked a good deal of punch without Joshua's able assistance.

"So Moses arose with his assistant Joshua, and Moses went up..."

– The Dream Author's Manual

I want to highlight that Joshua wasn't insecure and found no problem assisting Moses to move upwards. As a dream assistant with his own dream, Joseph knew that he will not miss out on his own manifestation just because you help someone else to pursue their dream. To the contrary, your dream fits into the other dream, and vice versa. Both work together to attain a higher level of perfection.

Joshua knew that to assist someone in realising their God-given vision is a privilege. I, too, count it an honour to be able to participate and contribute in helping you to reach your goal. This is why I do coaching. My aim in this book is to assist you to your own vision.

"There is no more noble occupation in the world than to assist another human being - to help someone succeed."

- **Alan Loy** (Author, Christian Psychotherapist)

15. D.U.M.B.™ PEOPLE ACHIEVE THEIR DREAMS

Have you ever heard the saying "I may be dumb, but I'm not stupid"? It sounds like a contradiction or an oxymoron, because dumb and stupid can mean one and the same thing. But I put it to you that being dumb is the way forward, and if you want to live your dreams, you better start acting dumb!

I rest my case on life. Most people who achieve their dreams and live their purpose fruitfully are not S.M.A.R.T at all. In fact, they are the very opposite: they are actually quite dumb. I know, it was a surprise to me too, until I studied their behaviour and attitudes. Think of any renowned, successful or significant person in history and I bet you they were are all dumb: Martin Luther King Jr., dumb. Bill Gates, dumb. Jesus Christ... DUMB!

At this point, you must be thinking Anthony-Lorenzo has really lost the plot! First, he is saying God is Not S.M.A.R.T! Now he is saying that Jesus is dumb and I must be dumb, too. Yes, that is exactly what I am saying and I encourage you to send the hate mail to my email address at the end of this book. But first let me explain. To be dumb means you appear to lack in intelligence or good judgment, and refrain from any or much speech. That description is quite fitting for the kind of behaviour we will be exploring as we move forward. As we have more than established, those who want to live their dreams do not act in what the world calls an intelligent or rational way.

Dumb people don't talk much; they let their actions speak for them. If Jesus Christ had chosen what seemed the intelligent thing to do and obeyed society's norms, would we have salvation available for all today? Of course not! When He was beaten and bruised, ridiculed, despised, He didn't utter a word, which would have seemed dumb to the people around Him who didn't understand His purpose. Jesus knew He would make a bigger impact by letting His actions of stretching His arms out wide, hanging on the cross for all of humanity, speak louder than any words could.

Here is the disclaimer. I said they were dumb, not stupid. Stupidity is a separate issue. It's not something that I support or condone.

When using the word dumb and not stupid, the message I want to get across is that you don't need to be a brainy guy like Albert Einstein to achieve your dreams. Yet you don't need to act like you have the brain of a fish either. All the dream pioneers were very self-aware and were in fact, intelligent in their own right. Yet it was not their intelligence that made them achieve what they did; it was their attitude.

Obviously, there is a point to all this dumb talk. And it's not about insulting you either. I just wanted to show you how, after studying the attitude and behaviour of many dream pioneers I came to understand that the way they lived formed the counter-acronym to S.M.A.R.T. - and that is D.U.M.B.

"Half of being smart is knowing what you are dumb about."

- **Solomon Short** (Writer)

16. D: IS FOR...

Have you ever wondered what is the magical ingredient that makes a dreamer excel? I could list a host of skills, abilities and character traits which can help or hinder you in your dream pursuit. These include communication, teamwork, initiative, problem solving, flexibility, computer skills and technical skills, among others. But out of them all, one stands out. The person who has it is simply outstanding. It is a 'must-have' for any and every dreamer. You have to possess, cultivate and put this skill into practice. Do you know which one it is yet? It's the habit of diligence. This came about by the thousands of stories about "ordinary" people who made an extraordinary impact. They laboured diligently so they could climb personal and professional heights they never believed were possible.

Diligence is a word that is foreign to many people. But this quality, more than any other, distinguishes a successful person from one who, let's say, wishes he was successful. Every Dream Pioneer had plenty of diligence.

Diligence is the continuous determined effort to accomplish a goal. It is being conscientious and persistent in any task you undertake. It is when your actions and work ethics reflect resolute and decisive carefulness. It is monitoring one's own activities to guard against idleness and carelessness.

A diligent person is hardworking and industrious, one who always tries his best no matter what the situation. Such people don't hesitate to do whatever is within their power to ensure that their dream happens. This underlying attitude is evident in all they think, say and do.

DREAMS ARE NOT MICROWAVE MEALS

"The soul of a lazy man desires, and has nothing; but the soul of the diligent shall be made rich."

– The Dream Author's Manual

Diligence is important because it is in direct opposition to human nature. The harsh reality is that very few will actually work hard enough and long enough to make their dream manifest, and be honoured as successful. This skill is uncommon by nature or nurture. In fact, we all tend to have a "microwave mentality". We want things quick, easy, and instant. We always choose the option that requires the least amount of effort. However, this is just another way of saying "I'm lazy". Laziness and procrastination are frequently and unfavourably commented on in The Dream Author's manual, in contrast to diligence. We have all come face to face with these obstacles in our own lives, at some point in time. Their chief danger lies in the fact that if you don't conscientiously deal with them, it proves that you don't want to work for your dream. If this is true, then maybe you are not worthy of it.

"Do you see a man diligent and skillful in his business? He will stand before kings; he will not stand before obscure men."

– The Dream Author's Manual

Suppose that you were interviewing a person who epitomised success to you. Never mind if it was someone who had a business empire or someone who is celebrating 25 years of marriage. Now, if you were to ask them to identify the secret of what made it work for them, guess what will more than likely come up? Hard work! They were minding their own business. In other words, their focus was on what concerns them. A dream pioneer must not be afraid of the term work, especially when it comes under the umbrella of diligence. Diligence is central to fulfilling your aspirations, whether you want to be an athlete, an actor or an entrepreneur. From building a church to writing a book, diligence is compulsory, not optional.

"A dream doesn't become reality through magic; it takes sweat, determination and hard work."

– **Colin Powell** (American statesman)

The saying goes, "Work smart, not hard." However, no matter what you choose to work at, you still have to WORK! You cannot get away from it. Plus, whoever thought working smart doesn't need hard work? Mental work or physical, you still need to exert energy. Albert Einstein, considered one of the smartest and most brilliant minds, once said, *"It's not that I'm so smart, it's just that I stay with problems longer."*

"The most practical, beautiful, workable philosophy in the world won't work – if you won't!"

Zig Ziglar (Author, salesman, and motivational speaker)

"I Can is 100 times more important than IQ."

– Unknown

Its great news for all of us without super IQ – diligence doesn't require IQ, but rather attitude. If you go hard at any task, it's only a matter of time before it will yield to you. This is what we call perseverance.

"Few things are impossible to diligence and skill. Great works are performed not by strength, but perseverance."

- Samuel Johnson (English writer)

DEVELOPING A DILIGENT ATTITUDE:

1. Laziness is for losers

Remind yourself that to win in life, you need to toss out laziness. Lazy people set themselves up to lose by default. Since they are never ready to put in the work required, their dream never works out. Look yourself in the eye to pinpoint the areas, times and things that trigger your inner "Homer Simpson". Then sit down and plan how you can break the pattern. Without diligence no dream ever succeeds.

2. Work purposefully

You need to know what you're sweating for. It's not just work but work with a purpose. You need to do and think only what will bring about a desired result which you have already foreseen. So think through what you want to see happen. Analyse how what you're doing now is helping you to make it happen. And if it's not – it's pointless and unproductive, and has no place in your life.

3. Daily diligence

Diligence is no flash in the pan. It's a long-distance run, a long haul. You school yourself decision by decision, action by action, to do it well and purposefully. You train yourself to be conscientious so your dream will be perfect in every detail. You create routine in your life so you have time to prepare for your day. This means you will be able to fine-tune your actions and decisions, to bring your dream to pass without wasting time or energy.

4. Examine yourself

Self-evaluation is about asking yourself "Am I being the best I can be?" and also, "Is this the best I can do?" As the saying goes, "Good, better, best; never let it rest until your good becomes better and your better, best!" Think and muse on what your best life looks like. Knowing that will bring out the desire and tenacity to stick with the things that bring out the best in you - even if they make you feel uncomfortable at first.

5. Be patient and persevere

Patience just means knowing for sure that your hard work will pay off one day if you persevere. As you sweat and suffer through the growth stages, you may have to accept that you will have to work longer and harder than others, but you're still right on track. So stay in your lane; you have to complete your own journey.

17.   U: IS FOR…

Being unwavering, which is another understated but vital key for a dreamer. Unwavering people recognise the value of having your own dream and the purpose attached to it.

Unwavering people are committed people; they are resilient and devoted to one thing. These people are marked by firm determination and resolution; they're immovable; they hold "firm convictions" and have "a firm mouth", with "steadfast resolve"; they're men or women who "don't ever give up, who don't waver in their loyalty".

The significance of being unwavering is impossible to overstress in the life of a Dreamer. Only one who never looks back or turns aside can withstand all the criticism and attacks of negative energy that come his way. Persevering without doubt enables you to carry on with determination despite temporary setbacks. Determination lets you stay strong in mind, which is where the battle is fought and won.

FIGHT BACK

Unwavering people have fighting spirit so they can punch back hard when life wallops them with a Tyson-like fist. These are the people who fight through all kinds of life stressors, whether job-related like work-life balance, unemployment, competition or changes in the way the job is done, or family problems such as divorce, illness, death, financial strain, relationship problems and so on. Regardless, they fight for a better outcome, knowing full well that the process may hurt them but they will still come out stronger and better.

THE POWER OF WORDS

Words are singularly the most powerful force available to humanity. We can choose to use this force constructively with words of encouragement, or destructively using words of despair. Words have energy and power with the ability to help, to heal, to hinder, to hurt, to harm, to humiliate and to humble.

- **Yehuda Berg** (Author, Clergyman)

Unwavering people are unshakeable. Indeed, they need to be because of the situations and people who cross them. You see, here and now we have people who can only be called, in street talk, "HATERS". One of the best interpretations of this term is an acronym that goes, "**H**aving **A**nger **T**owards **A**nyone **R**eaching **S**uccess". Like Dream Assassins, their words and deeds are directed at dissuading you from your dream. The way to stand against them is to have the rock-hard conviction that this is God's dream; you believe in yourself under God, that the vision of life you have been given will come to pass. No ill motive or discouraging words can counteract this faith. Your firm mouth will stand against the tide of negativity, because what lives in your mouth lives in your future. You have the power to create your world just by declaring it. This kind of power holds great responsibility and must not be taken for granted. The Dream Authors manual says "words kill, words give life; they're either poison or fruit – you chose". Choose your words wisely, and use them to bring your dream into being. Create a mantra or a positive confession that is conducive to your goals. An example of this could be:

"I am unstoppable, I am unwavering, I am constantly moving in the direction of my dreams"

This simple but powerful word said daily and often can make the world of difference.

The Unwavering Approach:

1. **Recognise there is no such thing as failure, only feedback**

Failure is not looking down but looking back with hope and positivity. Look at what went wrong so you can learn from it and develop a better approach. Reassess, adjust, and try again. Just like a professional boxer learns from every knock out, keep learning from every knock back!

2. Speak positively at all times

It is very important to realise that expressing surprise or dismay doesn't mean that you are giving up. You can acknowledge what has happened and yet continue to speak positively in the face of challenges, not allowing pessimism to overcome you.

3. Manage emotions

If you can't control your emotions they will control your decisions. So you need to choose right now that you are going to be the leader in your life. Don't let disappointments upset your emotional balance. Find ways to release stress without weakening your endurance, like working out, singing, reading or whatever you do at such times. Express your doubts constructively without damaging your confidence. Be sure you are going to overcome no matter how you feel - don't let your feelings rule your life.

4. Understand discomfort

Unwavering people recognise that the route to their dreams is often paved with discomfort and pain. Yet they also know that there is a purpose to it. A smoker knows that stopping will cause him some discomfort, but understands that it is a part of healing and growing into a better life.

5. Make up your mind

The people who achieve what they want in life are those who decided they will and nothing or no one can change that. In order to succeed, your desire for success should be greater than your fear of failure. Instead of wondering if you will be successful, decide YOU WILL be successful.

18.　　M: IS FOR...

Everyone knows those times when the fire flickers, and the spark of passion grows dim. You don't feel like you can bother with your dream any more. This experience seems to be part of the way we are. It may be that we allow our feelings to take charge.

Whatever the reason, you need to foresee this. This is when your motivation kicks in. Motivation is the tinder which makes the spark catch flame again. It is the fuel which keeps the fire glowing in the ashes. It is the petrol which keeps your car moving along. How F.A.R. would you get without it?

What is motivation? Motivation is stopping at the petrol station to refuel, and my advice is that you visit there every day. Without motivation, your car will slow down and stop. You'll find yourself headed off course, veering away from your dreams and your purpose. Before this happens, go to the petrol station and refill your tank. Use prayer and meditation to remember why you started in this direction and what's waiting for you at the end. Let new strength seep in to feed your mind, spirit and even your body, with things that are of real benefit.

"**Whatever is true, whatever is noble, whatever is right, whatever is pure, whatever is lovely, and whatever is admirable, if anything is excellent or praiseworthy, think about such things. Whatever you have learned... put it into practice!**"

- The Dream Author's Manual

When you spend time refueling, you'll go back to what stimulates you. You'll realise what you can do to provide a backup when your motivation levels begin to dip. This will re-focus you and re-commit you to effectively pursue your dream.

"**You are only as strong as your weakest thought.**"

– Tony Gaskins Jr. (Life Coach, Author)

IMAGINATION HAS PRACTICAL APPLICATION

Let me suggest some practical measures to keep yourself strong when you start to flag - even in your weakest thoughts. Your imagination is a powerful helper in this task. For example, create a dream diary that you can open up to remind yourself why you are doing what you are doing. This will ensure that your vision has been documented and that your mind stays focused.

"Write the vision and make it plain on tablets…"

- The Dream Author's Manual

Fortunately, today we don't need to go through the laborious task of engraving our vision on stone tablets. An internet tablet will do! Hey, if this is not an option, a simple ordinary pen and a notepad are just as good. It's all about writing down your vision, as a way to document it. It's about making it plain so you can remind yourself of what you felt and saw.

Many think that by 'plain' I mean 'specific'. No! 'Plain' just means that your dream is written down in a form which is basic, natural, easily read and understood. Just by writing it down, you have already set in motion the beginning of something great. It is like creating a contract with yourself for future achievement. Every time you read it and re-read it, your imagination will range wider in its delightful fields, and prompt new strategies to attain your dream.

"Imagination is more important than knowledge."

- **Albert Einstein** (German theoretical Physicist)

I read that the biggest nation in the world is not in either Africa or Asia. It is your very own imagiNATION. You can go, do and be everything and anything in your imagination. You can be anything according to the amazing things that are revealed in the Dream Author's book. He says…

"I, your Dream Author, working in partnership with you, am able to carry out my purpose and do superabundantly, far above and beyond all that you ask or think, infinitely beyond our highest prayers, desires, thoughts, hopes, or dreams."

Read your vision, breathe your vision, and own your vision. Why not? It is yours! Don't let a single day go by without basking in the golden radiance of your vision.

The journey to dream fulfilment is never going to be easy. It will be studded with moments of struggle and tension that can seem endless and hopeless. But keep reminding yourself that the Dream Pioneers who have gone before us went the same way. Their wonderful journey is well documented. They all won out to glory just because they didn't act S.M.A.R.T. If this path was good enough for them, it is good enough for us! What you need to do is to take positive action, reminding yourself that you are moving in the right direction, the one where your dream is leading you.

BECOMING MOTIVATED

1. **Keep Your Circle Tight**

Always keep close to people who help you keep your focus on your dream. Distance yourself from the negative influences in your life because, like it or not, they do affect your actions. Whether it is a relationship or an activity, if it doesn't help you follow your dream, out with it!

2. **Paying attention**

Keep your attention on what is important. This is not money, or the lack of it. It's not your starting position, good or bad. It's not your excuses or the people who surround you. People can drain your motivation away. They often go missing when you need their support. Even those whom you have helped and supported may not always be able or willing to show up during your journey. In fact, they may not even give you the time of day! But remember, before you make it, people will not pay you any attention. However, when you do make it, people will pay for your attention.

3. Remember Ever, Forget Never

Once you've committed yourself to pursuing your dream, and outlined a basic plan, you need to keep it in your sight and your thoughts all the time. It will constantly remind you of your goal and of what you need to do. Remember, out of sight is out of mind. Personally, I have a dream diary that I look through every day. It renews my inspiration, reminding me of what I want to accomplish and what I need to do.

4. Be proactive not reactive

When you're pursuing your dream, you don't wait for situations to crop up and then react to them. That would mean you're living in crisis, not in control. Instead, you turn the situations around to match your needs. You don't just sit around, waiting for things to happen; you're the kind who makes things happen!

5. Dream Pioneers

Mentors and role models are great sources of wisdom and inspiration for dream-followers. Always keep a look out for encouraging people who can guide you with seasoned maturity and experience. As The Dream Author's Manual says, **"In the multitude of counsel is safety."**

19. B: IS FOR...

"If you can believe, all things are possible to those who believe."

- The Dream Author's Manual

What a person believes is his own business, in general. But your beliefs shape your daily life to a great extent. What you believe is the root of your principles and values, your attitudes and ideals, and your overall philosophy for life. While belief looks and sounds like faith, there is a distinct and significant difference between them. I know this may come as a shock since most people use these words interchangeably. Yet, in the context of this book, the difference is small but highly relevant.

Belief works in partnership with faith. However, faith, as I use the term, is not based upon the information that you have about the world around you, but rather on what you know outside the field of your natural senses. Belief, however, is the result of received information and experience that you acknowledge as "fact". The result of that information is seen in the way you respond. To cite a somewhat strange example, when a police officer arrests someone they say, "I have reason to believe..." This tells us that belief comes from the information given and/or experienced; even more, belief is the result of reason. My question is: what are your grounds for belief?

"You can be anything you want to be, if you only believe with sufficient conviction and act in accordance with your faith; for whatever the mind can conceive and believe, the mind can achieve."

- Napoleon Hill

INFORMATION THAT FEEDS YOUR BELIEF

Imagination helps you believe. This is how it motivates you. You see, just as we saw earlier, information feeds the thought (belief).

Writer and novelist Michael Korda said this, *"To succeed, we must first believe that we can. If you don't believe that your dream is possible, guess what? It won't be! Even God who blessed you with the dream is limited... because He works in accordance to your belief level."*

This statement by Michael Korda carries great truth. When Jesus wanted to perform miracles in His hometown, he couldn't or chose not to, in response to what the people chose - not to believe in Him. Indeed, you receive as much - or as little - as you believe. If you don't believe God works miracles, you risk never seeing a miracle. The people of Jesus' hometown believed that he could not possibly do anything great because of who he was - a carpenter. This limited their outlook so that they were never destined to see the amazing things he did in other towns. So remember, beliefs are personal and not factual. They may be wrong or right; it is just a matter of how you interpret and whether you agree with the data.

This doesn't mean we can limit God. If He wants to do something, He can and will. But it will only happen if it agrees with His good purposes. When we see that Jesus Himself was limited by the unbelief of his own folks, we realise that we can prevent change in our own lives by denying that dream fulfilment is possible. By the way, believing in God is not the same as having faith in God. Many people believe in God; it's almost universal. But the Dream Author's manual says, **"You believe that there is one God; you do well; even the demons believe, and tremble".** Yes, even demons, bad people, those who kill in the name of God, may believe in God but never experience the actions of faith. This is why you need to start your dream journey with what you believe. You see, the reason that you believe lays the foundation of your faith.

(BE)LIEVING IN (YOU)RSELF

"To accomplish great things, we must not only act, but also dream; not only plan, but also believe."

- **Anatole France** (French poet, Journalist, and Novelist)

Look well at your beliefs and evaluate their validity and, relevance. Always be prepared to change them if they are ill-founded. For example, as children, we believed in the tooth fairy or in Father Christmas. Why? Because that's the information we were fed. I remember that when one of my teeth fell out, I was convinced the tooth fairy would leave me a present if I left my tooth under my pillow when I went to sleep. My mother had told me so; I'd seen and heard it on TV. How excited I was that night as I went to bed!

When the morning came, I woke up smiling with tooth missing. I looked eagerly for my present under my pillow. Guess what I found? My tooth! I was one shocked and disappointed child.

That's when I realised there are no tooth fairies. My belief changed. It wasn't relevant anymore; it didn't fit the facts. Of course, it was because my mum forgot her part in the illusion. This is why we need to re-evaluate what we believe from time to time. If what I believed today was just what I believed 15 years ago, I would be allowing the false information of 15 years ago to feed my thoughts. In that case, my faith would not have been strong enough to let me to write this book. As Tony Gaskins said, "You are only as strong as your weakest thought." Or I could say, believe what is right because your belief feeds your faith.

You need to have this crystal-clear. You see, what you believe determines who you believe in. You need to believe in yourself! This is non-negotiable. Most people never go beyond dreaming, not because their dream wasn't significant enough, but because they couldn't believe in themselves. If you are a dream pioneer, you need to understand that it's okay if others around you don't see what you do. It's fine if they can't see well enough to go beyond your "stretch". Only, you don't need to follow their belief. You need to move on, firm in your knowledge of who you are and what you're called to be. This is what Jesus did. Though he couldn't do anything in his own town, he moved on. He still knew who He was and whose He was – and it was more than a carpenter! As the Dream Author's manual says, *"Whatever you think about yourself, is what you are!"*

Believing in **You**rself is having the courage to BE YOU! Believing in yourself is just adapting your view of yourself to your dream. You believe you can do whatever you're called to do to attain your dream. You believe the potential is there and you realise it by faith.

Moses battled with a lack of self-belief, which he expressed by asking, "But what if they will not believe me?" What he was really saying was, "I don't believe in myself." This was at the root of the many excuses he offered God. He didn't want to expose himself to potential ridicule and embarrassment. But God did not accept his excuses. He knew who Moses was, and who he was going to become. Moses just needed to believe God's revelation for himself.

"Watch your thoughts, for they become words. Watch your words, for they become actions. Watch your actions, for they become habits. Watch your habits, for they become character. Watch your character, for it becomes your destiny."

- Unknown

HOW TO (BE) LIEVE IN (YOU) RSELF

1. **Attitude over Aptitude**

Your attitude breeds your outcome. Belief is an attitude, and your attitude to yourself is crucial to how you fulfil your dream. Have you noticed that even smart people can get stuck if their attitude is not right? Being able to see yourself as able to do whatever it takes to fulfil your dream is more important than being the most skilled, talented and capable person around. If your attitude is self-defeating, your talents might as well not exist. Your life will be a waste. So make sure you believe you can follow your dream. That winning attitude will lead you on to greatness.

2. Change your information

What goes in comes out. We live in an information age. News and knowledge bombards us from all sides. We eat this every day. Now hear this. What we receive as information changes our belief. And changed beliefs mean changed life. So if you need to believe the right things, change what you hear and see. Listen to motivational messages, read self-development books and meet inspiring dream pioneers. Make sure that whatever you connect with is a tool which will help you actualise your dream.

3. Be You

Have the courage to be you. Follow your natural bent. If you were born with a funny bone, be funny. If you have received a talent, shine! Don't hide it under a bushel. These natural tendencies are what give you your very own unique selling point (USP). They form the foundation of your personal brand. You do not need to be Superman to do something super. You just need to be proud of being yourself.

4. Give yourself permission to keep it moving

When things go wrong, as they inevitably will, don't get stuck on what you can't do or what didn't work. Negative brooding will only breed self-doubt. Give yourself permission to be human and to make mistakes. After all, you can only make an error if you make a move. If you've never made a mistake, you must be dead! So don't let disappointment be your permanent address.

5. Love yourself

For much of the time, your journey to your own star will be lonely. You need to be your own best friend. At times, it seems like we are our own worst enemy. We discourage ourselves and put ourselves down. But being your own best friend means loving yourself. You start with forgiving yourself and learning to like and highly appreciate your unique personality.

20. D.U.M.B. IS THE NEW SMART

I have presented a range of broad principles to inspire you with a new-old philosophy of dream fulfilment. I have tried to touch on a whole array of important concepts that will empower your attempt to live your dream and fulfil your purpose. Now, it's your turn to build upon them and create your own personalised, precise version. You've reached the starting line of your race.

There is irony in this book because I believe that the more D.U.M.B. you become, the smarter you become. As you start to act on D.U.M.B. advice, you will quickly realise it is the smartest thing you have ever done. Your results will amaze you because they are even better than you dared to expect.

Below is a summary of the key elements in this book. It is meant to remind you how to move past your S.M.A.R.T. barriers and live your dreams!

1. Acknowledge That You Have Dreams

Martin Luther King Jr. famously acknowledged it when he said, "I have a dream..." I have come across many people at work and outside who say that they don't have dreams. You know what? They actually do! Only, they just don't believe in them anymore because their "real life" gets in the way. They have buried their dreams alive.

2. Write Down Your Dreams

How can you live your dreams if you don't know what they are? Write them down, plain and clear. Don't critique them or wonder, "How can this happen?" Just do it!

3. Take Small Steps

Everything in life starts moving when you take the first step. You just have to get yourself moving in that direction, however small you start.

4. **(Faith + Action) = Results**

You need to have faith that you can follow your dream and fulfil it. You also need to get moving. As you fly with both wings beating synchronously, you will see your dream coming alive.

5. **Face The S.M.A.R.T. Barriers That Are Keeping You From Living Your Dreams**

What's keeping you from living your dreams? Not enough money? No time? Too many responsibilities? Know that none of these are the real barrier. Consider how you can overcome the obstacles. There will always be an excuse not to do something, but all you need is one good reason to do it!

6. **Watch out for your Dream Assassins and your Dream Assistants**

Figure out what role the people in your life play. Are they friends or foes? Whether they are friends, family, colleagues or teachers, you must identify to which side they belong because these relationships will play a vital part in your progress. If you discover a dream assassin, create distance between you and them. If they are dream assistants, stay close! No man is an island. Tell them how much you love and appreciate them. Enjoy their help. You do not want to live your dreams by yourself.

7. **Be DUMB**
It's the smartest move you could ever make!

21. GO CONFIDENTLY IN THE DIRECTION OF YOUR DREAMS

It is my conviction that you have made some sense out of your life after coming so far with me. The next step is yours. Do not disregard your life realities. That is neither helpful, nor possible. And living in denial is not delightful. Instead, you need to make your peace with your past and then let it go. Turn to the present and accept your dream completely. Embrace it with all your heart and soul. Commit yourself to go in the direction of your dream, with confidence that you will reach your place of fulfilment.

"Let go of the past and go for the future. Go confidently in the direction of your dreams. Live the life you imagined."

- **Henry David Thoreau** (Author, Philosopher, Abolitionist)

Of course, you probably know only too well how it feels to want something intensely while still being terrified to go for it. But do you realise that this fear limits what you can be? It restricts the impact you make on the world around you. It paralyses your progress. The only way out is to challenge your beliefs. If they imprison you, who taught them to you? What proof do you have that their beliefs are right? What reason is your belief based on? This process of reasoning will alter your beliefs for good. Your changed beliefs will transform your thinking. Instead of being a conformist, patterning yourself after the negative opinions, put-downs, and false expectations of those around you, you will become original, daring and creative. You will start to believe in what you are called to be. You need to let go and let God.

"Success doesn't come by knowing everything, but by knowing yourself."

- **Anthony-Lorenzo Brathwaite** (Author)

Remember, no one in the world knows everything about everything; not even Google! Universal knowledge is something only God has! All knowledge has its limits. Even so, you can be confident to move ahead with the abilities God has endowed you with. This is because knowledge, skill and power aren't the decisive factors.

"...The fastest runner doesn't always win the race, and the strongest warrior doesn't always win the battle. The wise sometimes go hungry, and the skillful are not necessarily wealthy. And those who are educated don't always lead successful lives. It is all decided by chance, by being in the right place at the right time."

- The Dream Author's Manual

Even the richest, most talented and capable people cannot predict or control everything that happens in their lives. They suffer loss and disappointment, ill-health and bad relationships like everyone else. No one, prince or pauper, royal or wretched, is immune from life. We all have good and bad times. So don't compare yourself to someone's standard; use your own. And never think you have succeeded because of the way you managed your life. It's all about God's confidence in you. Now on your marks, get set...

"GET AHEAD!"

REFERENCES:

1. The Dream Author's Manual

I do hope you have received help from *God is not S.M.A.R.T.,* in motivating and challenging you. However, the credit is not all mines. Most of the principles I used here have been taken directly from The Dream Author's manual for successful living. This book is also known as the "Good Book," and most commonly as the Bible. The Bible can be defined by the playful acronym **B**est **I**nstructions **B**efore **L**eaving **E**arth.

Definitions aside, the Bible is not like any other manuscript you have ever read. It doesn't inform, it equips. It is a rich resource which changes and actively guides you. I have read it, and I am still reading it, for the simple reason that each time around it shows me new ways and tools for successful living. And I'm not alone. The Bible has sparked huge undertakings of goodwill and friendliness, of compassion to the poor and downtrodden. It is the reason why thousands of hospitals have been built, multitudes fed and clothed, and orphanages founded.

Be warned: You will not be the same after you read this book.

2. 'Lewis Hamilton just happy to live the dream' retrieved from http://www.timesonline.co.uk/tol/sport/formula_1/article5076874.ecedate retrieved: April 2010

3. References from the Dream Author's Manual

PART ONE: THE DREAM AUTHOR, THE DREAMER, AND THE DREAM

The Dream Author
- Psalm 139:16-17 (Amp)
- Job 33:14-18
- Eccl. 11:4,6 (ERV)
- Isaiah 55:8 (Msg)

If there's no purpose, there's no point!
- Ecclesiastes 3:1 (NKJV)

Dream Pioneers
- Hebrews 12:1-3 (Msg)

Life Out Loud (LOL)
- James 4:14 (NKJV)
- Eph 5:11-16 (MSG)
-

How FAR Do You Want To Go?
- Hebrews 11:1 (Amp)
- Ecclesiastes 8:17

God is not S.M.A.R.T.!
- Romans 12:2

God is not Specific
- Hebrews 11:8
- Numbers 23:19 (NIV)

God is not Measurable
- Proverbs 16:3 (Amp)
- Proverbs 19:21
- I Samuel 16:7b

God is not Attainable
- Ecclesiastes 11:4-6 (NKJV)

God is not Realistic
- Mark 10:27 (NKJV)

God is not Time-bound
- 2 Peter 3:8
- Gen 4:3
- Ecclesiastes 3:1-8
- Habakkuk 2: 3 (CEV)

God is not S.M.A.R.T.! God is Wise!
- 1 Tim 1:17
- Proverbs 3:5-7

PART TWO: GET UP, GET GOING & GETAHEAD

Arise and Shine
- Isaiah 60:1 (Amp, Msg)

Dream Assistants
- Numbers 11:28 (NKJV)
- Exodus 24:13

D is for...

- Proverbs 13:4
- Proverbs 22:29 (Amp)

M is for...
- Phil 4:8-9
- Habakkuk 2:2-3

B is for...
- Mark 9:23
- Romans 10:17
- Mark 6:4-6
- James 2:19, (NKJV)

Go confidently in the direction of your dreams
- Ecclesiastes 9:11 (NLT)

ABOUT THE AUTHOR: ANTHONY-LORENZO

Anthony-Lorenzo is an influential educator, charismatic entertainer and ambitious entrepreneur, who has been making a positive impact through these mediums for over 10 years. His energetic, engaging and eccentric personality means he is naturally able to connect with audiences across the spectrum.

Over time, Anthony-Lorenzo has become a sought-after and popular personality who has been featured guest on radio, in magazines, guest panels and social events. He has a growing following across social media platforms with an active online presence.

Anthony-Lorenzo started from very humble beginnings and according to social norms he could've been labelled a statistical failure, a community outcast, and educationally poor. Yet through his rich spirit, diligent attitude and powerful faith, he is proving that people and problems cannot override your purpose.

Website: Anthony-Lorenzo.com
Facebook: AnthonyLorenzo
Twitter: @iAmTonyLorenzo
Instagram: @iAmTonyLorenzo